CONSERVATIVE CHRISTIAN IDENTITY & SAME-SEX ORIENTATION

PETER LANG
New York • Washington, D.C./Baltimore • Bern
Frankfurt am Main • Berlin • Brussels • Vienna • Oxford

RICK PHILLIPS

CONSERVATIVE CHRISTIAN IDENTITY & SAME-SEX ORIENTATION

The Case of Gay Mormons

PETER LANG
New York • Washington, D.C./Baltimore • Bern
Frankfurt am Main • Berlin • Brussels • Vienna • Oxford

Library of Congress Cataloging-in-Publication Data

Phillips, Rick.
Conservative Christian identity and same-sex orientation:
the case of gay Mormons / Rick Phillips.
p. cm.
Includes bibliographical references and index.
1. Homosexuality—Religious aspects—Church of Jesus Christ of Latter-day Saints.
2. Homosexuality—Religious aspects—Mormon Church. 3. Church of Jesus
Christ of Latter-day Saints—Doctrines. 4. Mormon Church—Doctrines. I. Title.
BX8643.H65P39 261.8'35766—dc22 2004014242
ISBN 0-8204-7480-0

Bibliographic information published by **Die Deutsche Bibliothek**.
Die Deutsche Bibliothek lists this publication in the "Deutsche
Nationalbibliografie"; detailed bibliographic data is available
on the Internet at http://dnb.ddb.de/.

Cover design by Joni Holst

The paper in this book meets the guidelines for permanence and durability
of the Committee on Production Guidelines for Book Longevity
of the Council of Library Resources.

275 Seventh Avenue, 28th Floor, New York, NY 10001
www.peterlangusa.com

Printed in Germany

Table of Contents

ACKNOWLEDGMENTS

A number of people provided assistance and support as I worked on this project. Several colleagues at Utah State University read and critiqued an earlier version of this work, including Gary Kiger, Pamela Riley, and Steven Simms. Richley Crapo, an expert on both Mormonism and the cross-cultural study of homosexuality, was an invaluable resource and a sharp critic throughout the research and writing process. Richley alerted me to several important sources for this study, and brought an anthropologist's eye to the process of ethnographic research among gay Mormons. Without his help this book could not have been written.

Wayne Brekhus at the University of Missouri read and commented on an early draft of this book, and provided a number of important insights on the formation of gay identities. O. Kendall White of Washington and Lee University and Daryl White of Spelman College entertained my questions about Mormonism, and agreed to lend their expertise to this project.

I have also enjoyed support from my colleagues in the Department of Sociology, Anthropology and Criminal Justice at the University of North Florida. Ron Lukens-Bull provided encouragement and advice through the final editing and production of the manuscript. Scott Frey cheerfully accommodated my unorthodox scheduling requests so that classroom duties wouldn't keep me away from my writing. Finally, I thank my wife, Jany. Whenever things get difficult I can always count on her optimism to keep me going.

I have tried to be precise and treat the subject matter fairly throughout this book. In spite of this, I am sure that certain shortcomings remain. I alone am responsible for these.

CHAPTER ONE
HOMOSEXUALITY AND MORAL ENTREPRENEURS

This book is a sociological study of homosexuals and homosexuality in the Church of Jesus Christ of Latter-day Saints—the LDS, or Mormon church. Homosexuality within Mormonism is interesting to sociologists because the LDS church, like many conservative churches in the United States, demands a high degree of conformity, loyalty and obedience from its members. And, like most conservative churches, Mormonism also regards homosexuality as abnormal, and views homosexual relations as sinful. The Mormon church is an important protagonist in the battle between gay rights groups and conservative Christians to define and control homosexuality in the United States. Aside from its rigid stance on the issue, the church is one of the nation's largest Protestant denominations, and wields considerable political power in the western U.S.[1] The church also possesses vast wealth, and uses its resources to lobby politicians and shape public opinion about issues relating to homosexuality.[2]

Sociologists have long observed that people use religious beliefs to construct their worldview and order their reality, yet also note that sexuality, or sexual preference, is an essential element of one's identity. Thus, the homosexual Mormon is caught between two conflicting statuses, both of which are often highly salient. On the one hand, the person is sexually attracted to members of his or her same sex, and, on the other, the person can possess strong religious beliefs and deep spiritual convictions that make it difficult for him or her to leave the church. This book attempts to show how people who hold these two incongruent statuses struggle to reconcile the contradictions in their lives. It also examines how the church's stand on the issue of homosexuality has evolved through contact with its gay members and through interfacing with the larger society. First, however, it is necessary to outline the nature of sociology's relationship with the study of homosexuality, and present some key theoretical concepts that will inform my analysis.

Sociology and Homosexuality

In the first half of the 20th century, many influential sociologists regarded homosexuality as social pathology. According to this view, deviation from "consensual" sexual norms is a social sickness, and those who would engage in sexual practices abhorred by society are seen as deviants—offenders of the normative order. Because most people are heterosexual, sociologists made a *prima facie* case for heterosexuality as normal and functional, and by implication, homosexuality as abnormal and dysfunctional. Unfortunately, this case is a *non sequitur*.

Philosophers who have observed the social world have long recognized the temptation to equate what *is* with what *ought* to be. Many social scientists have succumbed to this temptation, concluding that because people often seem to be successful in organizing themselves in certain ways, or in attaining certain social goals, that that organization is necessarily good or right, and those goals are noble and virtuous.[3] It was Hume, however, who first demonstrated that an *is* does not infer an *ought*, noting in essence that, "depending on how far you push the equation ought=is, it would justify the most heinous and bizarre acts."[4] Known to philosophy as the *Naturalistic Fallacy*, the mistake of equating *is* with *ought* has been especially manifest in the social sciences. Throughout the history of social science, practitioners have observed the typical, inferred that the typical is "normal," and further concluded that what is "normal" is good. Myers writes:

> No survey of human behavior—say of sexual practices—logically dictates what is "right" behavior. If most people do it, that does not make it right. There is no way we can move from objective statements of fact to prescriptive statements of what ought to be without injecting our values. ... In such ways, both obvious and subtle, social [scientists'] personal values influence their work.[5]

Unfortunately, with regard to the study of deviance, sociologists have been slow learners. What Hume understood in the 1760s did not dawn upon most sociologists until the 1960s. Thomas Kuhn has demonstrated that the prevailing intellectual climate of the day shapes scientific inquiry, and even circumscribes the questions that scientists can ask—sociologists included.[6] Thus, it is a paradox (and perhaps an embarrassment) that the forces of society hid the *subjective* nature of sexual norms from the very "science" of society. Sociology, then, was so immersed in the social order of the day that many of the processes of that order remained hidden from even the most brilliant minds in the discipline.

But the social upheaval of the 1960s began to change all this. As various oppressed groups—African-Americans and women, for example—began to vigorously challenge the "accepted," "consensual" social order, sociologists were shaken from their slumber. The notions of social conflict and hegemony—ideas with a long history in the discipline—began to supplant "function" in sociological theories as the essential elements of human society. Sociologists began to realize that deviance is, in actuality, a social construction, and that definitions of deviance are imposed on society by powerful interest groups seeking to serve their own interests. The emphasis began to shift from examining deviants themselves to examining how things become seen and *labeled* as deviant. Situations and social contexts joined people as units of analysis in studies of deviant behavior. For the first time, homosexuality was analyzed as a category of deviance that is neither right nor wrong. By the time the 1960s were over, the "labeling perspective" was one of the most influential theoretical orientations in sociology, dominating the sociology of deviance.

Labeling Perspective: The Ownership of Deviance

The labeling perspective, or labeling theory, achieved prominence in the late 1960s—a time of normative upheaval in the United States. First and foremost, the perspective is a critique of the functionalist explanation of social deviance and the functionalist practice of viewing deviance as an objective disorder. Labeling theorists depart from functionalists in that they are just as concerned with the people who *make* the rules as they are with the people who *break* the rules. Becker writes:

> It is an interesting fact that most scientific research and speculation on deviance concerns itself with people who break rules rather than with those who make and enforce them. If we are to achieve a full understanding of deviant behavior, we must get these two possible foci of inquiry into balance.[7]

Becker asserts that the functionalist view begs the interesting sociological question: Why this set of norms and not some other?

> [The traditional view in sociology] defines deviance as the infraction of some agreed upon rule. It then goes on to ask who breaks rules, and to search for the factors in their personalities and life situations that might account for the infractions. ... Such an assumption seems to me to ignore the central fact about deviance: it is created by society.[8]

Labeling theorists like Becker propose that categories of deviance are subjective phenomena. They assert that defining deviance is the province of powerful persons and interest groups who make rules and brand those who break these rules as deviants in order to further their political aims, protect their power, extend their influence, and enhance their prestige. Hence, before a particular status or behavior can be viewed by society as deviant, and before those holding this status or engaging in this behavior can be labeled as "deviants," someone, or some group, must construct rules which are legitimated—through consensus, force, or otherwise—that define the behavior in question as morally wrong. Thus, as Becker succinctly concludes: "The deviant is one to whom that label has been successfully applied; deviant behavior is behavior that people so label."[9]

Becker calls those who attempt to define new categories of deviance and label new social problems "moral entrepreneurs." Moral entrepreneurs are kept in business by their vested interests and values. Since the issues they attempt to label usually have some significance for members of society, these moral crusaders typically have similar groups that serve as allies, and are also usually opposed by other moral entrepreneurs.[10]

Moral Entrepreneurs

One need only open a newspaper or turn on the television in the United States today to see the lengths to which moral entrepreneurs will go to legitimize their definition of homosexuality. Conservative political and religious groups seek to convince the public that homosexuality is unnatural, sinful and a threat to American values. Attempts to impose this definition of homosexuality have reached the highest echelons of power in this nation.

While religious groups in this camp argue with vigor that homosexuality is a sin that is condemned by the Bible, their secular counterparts complain that the acceptance of homosexuality would increase the spread of AIDS, allow homosexuals to recruit children into gay lifestyles, destroy the institution of marriage, and erode the power and morale of the United States military. These moral entrepreneurs see those concerned with "gay rights" as individuals in search of "special rights" and do not believe that these should be conferred upon a group organized around sexual orientation.

The violence against gay people in this country is ample evidence that a definition of homosexuality as unnatural and undesirable has struck a resonant chord with many members of the American public. But like any divisive issue, there is more than one interest group attempting to define homosexuality. The gay rights movement also qualifies as a moral entrepreneur and has been very active in asserting its definition as well. Calling homosexuality an "alternate lifestyle," gay activists and allied groups stress that the vast majority of homosexuals are normal, law abiding citizens who are capable of loving, long-term relationships and who can be trusted in their jobs and as parents just like heterosexuals. They urge tolerance and push legislators to enact laws that prohibit discrimination against men and women on the basis of sexual orientation. Presently, the gay rights movement wields considerable political power in the United States.

Moral entrepreneurs who seek to label homosexuality as an acceptable, alternative lifestyle cite numerous studies in the fields of psychiatry and psychology to demonstrate that homosexuality cannot be changed through therapy, that homosexuality is not chosen, and that homosexuals are not more poorly adjusted mentally than their heterosexual counterparts.

The amassed literature to substantiate these claims is impressive. As early as the 1950s, Evelyn Hooker demonstrated that even skilled psychiatrists could not tell a homosexual from a heterosexual based solely on a psychiatric profile—something that did not bode especially well for a discipline that, at that time, characterized homosexuality as a mental disorder and the result of a disturbed upbringing. Hooker's research was followed by other studies that concluded that homosexuals did not suffer more mental health problems than their heterosexual counterparts, and that homosexuality should no longer be characterized as a mental disorder.[11]

Armed with this research, the gay rights movement lobbied the American Psychiatric Association (a third moral entrepreneur with *its* vested interests and labeled categories of deviance)[12] to remove homosexuality from among the mental disorders listed in the third edition of its *Diagnostic and Statistical Manual of Mental Disorders*. After bitter and acrimonious debate, the APA finally agreed to remove homosexuality from the DSM III-R in 1974. This constitutes a major victory for the gay rights movement and an act of skillful moral entrepreneurialism.

Since 1974, the gay rights movement has posted many impressive gains. But with each new step forward, the backlash from moral crusaders in the conservative camp grows more insistent. American culture is a battleground in an all-out war for the privilege of labeling homosexuality, with combatants trading frequent and telling blows in the public arena. The political maelstrom surrounding homosexuality shows no sign of abating. Considering the powerful emotions on both sides, it seems increasingly likely that the present stalemate and war of words will persist for the foreseeable future. This ideological standoff creates an interesting situation in the United States. The present state of moral pluralism in America creates a buyers market for citizens, who are free to choose, within the limits of their socialization, which definition of homosexuality they find more convincing.

Labeling and the Individual

Aside from labeling various ideas and activities as deviant, moral entrepreneurs seek to label the people espousing these ideas or engaging in these activities as deviants as well. The consequences of bearing a stigmatized label have been recognized for some time in sociology. In the first complete delineation of the labeling perspective, Edwin Lemert argues that at first deviants resist the labels that are applied (or misapplied) to them. Nevertheless, in spite of their efforts to reject the label and the accompanying stigma that now characterizes them, "deviants" often find that because their opportunities in society are restricted by those who equate them with their label, they are forced into stereotypical behavior.[13] The classic example of this is the boy who has been labeled delinquent. When other parents in the neighborhood forbid their children to play with such a boy because of his label, he is forced to associate with others who bear the same stigma. It is no surprise to labeling theorists that delinquent behavior often persists in such instances.

In time, individuals bearing a stigmatized label become resigned to the label's permanence and weight. Elements of the label then become incorporated into the deviant's personality, and he or she begins to see him- or herself in terms of the label just as others do. Goffman writes: "given that the stigmatized individual in our society acquires identity standards which he applies to himself in spite of failing to conform to them, it is inevitable that he will feel some ambivalence about his own self."[14] Hence, the label becomes internalized.

A negative label often becomes the most salient status an individual possesses. Sometimes the deviant's life is completely rearranged and his or her social interactions totally redefined by the label. Becker calls such labels "master statuses" and points out, "Some statuses, in our society as in others, override all other statuses and have a certain priority. ... The status of deviant (depending on the kind of deviance) is this kind of master status."[15] Such a master status can be as integral to a person's identity as gender, race or national origin. Homosexuality is an archetypal master status. This does not, of course, mean that the process of labeling causes homosexuality, but rather that once the accouterments of the label "homosexual" have been successfully applied, the social interactions of homosexual people revolve around this essentializing label.

Homosexuals in Christian Churches

To this point, we have outlined two major labels given to homosexuals and their lifestyles by moral entrepreneurs in America. While regional variables and socialization processes seem to be strongly related to which of these labels people are likely to support, it is also likely that the prominence and high visibility of both camps provides ample opportunity for many individuals to choose which definition best suits them and their circumstances. This is also true for homosexuals themselves. Hence, those with same sex attractions, tempered by their socialization and social conditions, may ally themselves with whichever label seems to fit their worldview and profit them most. It is hardly surprising that most seem to prefer the label offered by the gay rights movement and other groups sympathetic to gays.

In spite of this, many gay people often find themselves in occupations or other social situations where conditions strongly favor the other, "conservative" view of same sex relationships. When this happens, there is often conflict between the two incongruent roles. Such conflict can place a strain on one's identity.[16] For instance, Woodman points out that managing a homosexual identity is often difficult for college students because the expectation of heterosexual behavior is strong among young people of this age.[17] Almaguer argues that Hispanic men often have a difficult time harmonizing the expectations for gender role behavior that accompany the Latino notion of "machismo" with a homosexual orientation.[18] In the occupational sphere, the problems facing gays in the United States military are well known and widely publicized. And Lienen writes that gay policemen have difficulty dealing with contradictions between the gender role expectations that accompany being a police officer and those that accompany being a homosexual.[19]

Managing one's homosexuality is especially difficult for gay members of Christian churches. Certain Christian groups are among the most vocal supporters of a conservative definition of homosexuality. Gay people who wish to avoid being branded with this conservative label, but who nevertheless wish to remain involved and active in Christianity, must choose from among those few denominations that extend the hand of fellowship to homosexuals.

Some gay Christians, however, have internalized the notion of homosexuality as sinful and deviant. Although many are well aware of the claims and arguments of the gay rights movement, there are some who, despite their own sexual preference, continue to hold the view that homosexuality is a perversion and that a homosexual lifestyle is an abomination before God. Most who see themselves this way do so because of their lifelong affiliation with fundamentalist or evangelical Christian groups.

This paradox, of course, begs several questions: why would anyone *want* to be labeled as a sinful deviant? Why would someone *choose* to affiliate with a conservative Christian group when other, more accepting religious groups are readily available? The answer to these questions is that conservative religious groups are very effective moral entrepreneurs, and are quite good at making their labels stick.

Religions as Moral Entrepreneurs

Moral entrepreneurs want to label certain categories of deviance and control the rules that govern which behaviors are considered deviant. Religions have always been especially active as moral entrepreneurs, and have been the leaders in such moral crusades in America as the fight against (and for) slavery, the abortion debate, and the temperance movement. Becker states:

> Many moral crusaders have strong humanitarian overtones. The crusader is not only interested in seeing to it that other people do what he thinks is right. He believes that if they do what is right it will be good for them. Or he may feel that his reform will prevent certain kinds of exploitation of one person by another.[20]

Religions have always attempted to define the rules governing sexual behavior in this country, and legal prohibitions against homosexuality have tended to mirror those prescribed in the Bible.

Religious movements are good at applying their labels because for many, their edicts are legitimated by the force and power of God. Those who use the Bible to define proper sexual conduct cannot be countered by logical arguments or scientific evidence. Rather, conservative churches use appeals to the supernatural to convince the faithful that church edicts reflect divine will. Because of this, followers are more likely to internalize the labels that these groups impose. Peter Berger writes:

> Let the institutional order be so interpreted as to hide, as much as possible, its constructed character. Let that which has been stamped out of the ground *ex nihilo* appear as the manifestation of something that has been existent from the beginning of time, or at least from the beginning of this group. Let the people forget that this order was established by men and continues to be dependent upon the consent of men. ... In sum: Set religious legitimations.[21]

Conservative religions are also able to exact great conformity from their members by placing strict limitations on their behavior and heavy demands on their time. Such demands are difficult and costly for followers, but also provide great rewards in the form of shared norms and a sense of community. Sociologists argue that the order and meaning strict churches provide produces high levels of religious conviction and devotion.[22] Thus, for gay people raised within these sects, their religious identity often becomes one "master status" while their homosexuality constitutes another, incompatible one. Such status conflict can often be intense and difficult to manage.

The Mormon Church as Moral Entrepreneur

This book presents a study of how one conservative religious group—The Church of Jesus Christ of Latter-day Saints (the LDS, or Mormon, church)—labels homosexuality and how homosexual members of this church are managed within it. It is informed by the general tenets of the labeling perspective, and seeks to outline the way the church as a moral entrepreneur advances its view that homosexuality is deviant. It also charts the reluctant compromises evident in the evolution of the church's policies for managing homosexual members as the organization tries to fend off the gains posted by competing moral entrepreneurs in the gay rights movement.

In addition to examining the institutional church, this book also examines the lives of gay Mormons themselves. It offers answers to the questions: How do gay Mormons acquire and internalize their deviant label in the church? And, how do they manage the label once it is applied?

I approach these questions by breaking down the church's label of homosexuality into two fairly distinct elements: (1) an actual definition of homosexuality, which regards homosexuals as flawed and abnormal, and (2) a set of acceptable, church approved behaviors for homosexuals within the church which include: changing (or attempting to change) one's sexual orientation from homosexual to heterosexual, marrying heterosexually to "cure" homosexuality, and living a celibate lifestyle without sexual expression of any kind, including masturbation.

The gay Mormons I studied had a variety of responses to the LDS church's definition of homosexuality and its behavioral mandates for gay members. Some had internalized the belief that homosexuality is deviant, and followed the admonition to eschew homosexual relations. Others accepted the church's view, but nevertheless maintained secret relationships with same-sex partners—something that often filled them with guilt. Another group of informants rejected the church's definition of homosexuality, but abstained from same-sex relations, hoping that their faithfulness and obedience would convince church leaders to eventually accept them as they are. Finally, a few of my informants actively resisted the church, and lobbied openly for change. These gay Mormon activists rejected the notion that homosexuality is deviant, and saw nothing inherently immoral about gay relationships.

These various adaptive strategies fit neatly within a four-part typology based on whether or not a gay Mormon has internalized the church's definition of homosexuality, and on how closely that person lives their lives in accordance with the church's behavioral standards. This typology is displayed in Table 1.1 on the following page.

Plan of the Book

I begin the analysis by introducing the history of the Mormon church's theological and social reaction to homosexuality in chapters two and three. Following this, chapter four examines how one assumes a gay identity within Mormonism, and the experience of "coming out" in the church. Chapter five introduces those who accept the church's definition of homosexuality, and describes the struggles of those who adopt this identity management strategy. Chapter six recounts the experiences of those who still desire to remain within the LDS church, but who nevertheless reject the church's claims that homosexuality is sinful and flawed. Finally, chapter seven deals with those who cannot reconcile homosexuality and Mormonism, and choose suicide instead.

TABLE 1.1 IDENTITY MANAGEMENT STYLES OF GAY MORMONS

STRATEGY FOR IDENTITY MANAGEMENT	ATTITUDE TOWARD CHURCH DEFINITION OF HOMOSEXUALITY	ACCEPTANCE OF CHURCH PRESCRIBED BEHAVIOR FOR HOMOSEXUALS
Living a celibate lifestyle, marrying heterosexually, changing sexual orientation (Chapter Five)	ACCEPTS	ACCEPTS
Resigning oneself to church condemnation (Chapter Five)	ACCEPTS	REJECTS
Seeking reform of church policies while still accepting church behavioral standards (Chapter Six)	REJECTS	ACCEPTS
Seeking reform of church policy while rejecting church behavioral standards (Chapter Six)	REJECTS	REJECTS

Methodology

Before proceeding with the analysis, it is necessary to comment on how this study was done. Reliable data on Mormon homosexuals is difficult to come by. There is no sampling frame available for more traditional methods of sociological research, and there is very little in the way of sociological literature that can serve as a guide for developing research questions. For these reasons, this study is an exploratory study, describing a group of people who have never been the subject of sociological research before.

Like many field studies in deviance, this study began when I became aware of a "deviant" social group worthy of ethnographic analysis. In the course of my ongoing inquiry into the sociology of Mormonism, I came across an item in a journal for Mormon scholarship announcing the existence of a support group for gay Mormons. I was intrigued, recognizing immediately from my own Mormon upbringing the contradictions inherent in being Mormon and being gay. One day I brought this news item to the attention of several gay friends who were active in the gay community at a large northern Utah university. To my surprise, they were familiar with this support group. They also informed me that several members of the campus Gay and Lesbian Alliance were still active[23] members of the LDS church. Ever the curious sociologist, I asked if arrangements could be made for me to meet these men. Phone calls were made, and I was introduced the next day to three men who were gay, LDS, and *very* religious. During the course of our informal conversations, I inquired as to how they reconciled their sexual preference with their religious affiliation. I was astounded by their answers, and even more amazed by their stories of how they became aware of their homosexuality, and how Mormon ecclesiastical authorities had dealt with them when their sexual preference became known within the church. Shortly after these initial interviews, I decided to write an ethnography of Mormon homosexuals, and this study was born.

Using these men as key informants, I used a snowball sample to find other gay Mormons. I also joined the gay Mormon support group and began attending their monthly meetings and reading the literature they produced. I interviewed the leaders of several chapters of this group, and in each instance asked the individual being interviewed to refer me to other gay Mormons who would be willing to participate in the study.

In addition to the information unearthed by my informants, I learned of the existence of a "gay underground" at church-owned Brigham Young University, and spent a week living with and interviewing these men and their friends. I also attended community gay rights functions, the meetings of gay student groups on other local college campuses, and many other gathering points where interesting informants were likely to be found. Sometimes I was nosy, but more often than not the people I encountered were eager to be part of a study and usually had more to say than I had time to hear.

About the time I had determined that my research was done and the data were ready to analyze, I became intrigued with persistent rumors of gay Mormons who were married, those who lived celibate, and those who claimed to have changed from gay to straight. Up until now, I had only encountered men who were more or less out of the closet. I had yet to meet those who accepted the church's definition of homosexuality as sinful and flawed. I began to hunt for these individuals in earnest. They were very difficult to find and rather reluctant to submit to interviews. My search took me to numerous gay bars and gay "pick-up points," to conferences for people desiring to "change" their sexual orientation, and to numerous LDS single adult social functions throughout Utah.

This time, my interviews progressed according to what Denzin calls the "non-schedule standardized interview"—an extremely flexible interview design that is geared to get certain information from every respondent, but allows the researcher considerable latitude to explore topics of interest.[24] I asked respondents about their level of religiosity, their family's religiosity, and whether or not they had served an LDS mission. I asked them about their "coming out" experiences, and how they reconciled being gay with LDS theology.

Seventy-one interviews were obtained for the study. Care was taken to ensure that all gay Mormon lifestyles outlined in this book were about equally represented, even though the temptation to interview many more of the easy to find "out of the closet" types was hard to resist. The earliest research design for this study provided for lesbian Mormon women to be interviewed as well as gay men. A few were discovered and interviewed, but it became apparent that their experiences and the church's reactions to them were very different from those of their male counterparts. Given that the study was financed from my own limited resources, I decided with some regret to limit the analysis to gay men in the church.

For clarification and insight, I also interviewed several counselors at LDS Social Services and a number of bishops and former bishops. These men provided excellent balance and helped me understand the church's rationale for its policies. Some were concerned that I was writing an anti-Mormon book, but agreed to chat with me when I assured them that I would try to be fair to the church. Some consented to be interviewed only after reading early drafts of chapters two and three. Others declined to be interviewed after perusing the same chapters. Lastly, I spoke to a number of the parents and siblings of my informants to get a feel for how a family member's homosexuality impacts a devout Mormon family.

Reliability and Validity

Venturing onto sociological *terra incognita* is an exciting enterprise, but poses considerable problems for ensuring a study's reliability and validity. The most problematic issue to address, of course, is the sample. Obviously, one has no way of knowing how representative of gay Mormons as a whole the selected sample is. For this reason, generalizations and categorizations made from my interviews must be treated as anecdotal. Nevertheless, I took pains to ensure that the data were consistent, and that gay Mormons from all points of view were sampled fairly equally. Informants sometimes contradicted each other, but the overall level of agreement among them was quite remarkable, particularly with respect to the way the official church reacted to their homosexuality.

One other methodological tool I employed to enhance the study's validity was the use of the Weberian concept of *verstehen*. Max Weber defined verstehen as a researcher's ability to gain insights into the behavior of research subjects by looking at situations from their perspective and through their eyes. According to Theodorson and Theodorson, "The success of the method of verstehen depends on the observer's understanding of the culture and social norms within which the behavior being observed occurs."[25] I claim the appropriate use of verstehen by virtue of my lifelong affiliation with the LDS church and typical rigorous upbringing and indoctrination in the unique culture and theology of Mormonism. This, in many instances, provided the kind of insight and understanding that would certainly be lost on a researcher unfamiliar with the Mormon worldview.

Notes

1. Barry A. Kosmin, Egon Mayer and Ariela Keysar, *American Religious Identification Survey, 2001* (New York: The Graduate Center of the City University of New York, 2001).
2. D. Michael Quinn, "Prelude to the National 'Defense of Marriage' Campaign: Civil Discrimination against Feared or Despised Minorities," *Dialogue: A Journal of Mormon Thought* 33, no. 3 (2000): 1–52.
3. Ed Miller, *Questions that Matter* (New York: McGraw-Hill, 1984).
4. Ibid., 387.

5. David G. Myers, *Social Psychology* (New York: McGraw-Hill, 1993), 11. Emphasis in original.
6. Thomas Kuhn, *The Structure of Scientific Revolutions* (Chicago: University of Chicago Press, 1962).
7. Howard S. Becker, *Outsiders* (New York: The Free Press, 1963), 163.
8. Ibid., 8.
9. Ibid., 9.
10. Charles H. McGaghy, *Deviant Behavior: Crime, Conflict, and Interest Groups* (New York: Macmillan, 1985), 101.
11. Evelyn Hooker, "The Adjustment of the Male Overt Homosexual," *Journal of Projective Techniques* 21 (1957): 18–31. See also Judd Marmor, *Homosexual Behavior: A Modern Reappraisal* (New York: Basic Books, 1980).
12. See Horwitz, Allan V., *Creating Mental Illness*. Chicago: University of Chicago Press, 2003.
13. Edwin Lemert, *Social Pathology: Approach to the Theory of Sociopathic Behavior* (New York: McGraw-Hill, 1951).
14. Erving Goffman, *Stigma: Notes on the Management of a Spoiled Identity* (Englewood Cliffs, NJ: Prentice Hall, 1963), 106.
15. Becker, *Outsiders*, 33.
16. Wayne Brekhus, *Peacocks, Chameleons, Centaurs: Gay Suburbia and the Grammar of Social Identity* (Chicago: University of Chicago Press, 2003).
17. Natalie Jane Woodman, "Mental Health Issues Relevant to Lesbian Women and Gay Men," *Journal of Gay and Lesbian Psychotherapy* 1, no. 1 (1989): 53–63.
18. Thomas Almaguer, "Chicano Men: A Cartography of Homosexual Identity and Behavior," *Differences* 3, no. 1 (1991): 75–100.
19. Stephen Lienen, *Gay Cops* (New Brunswick, NJ: Rutgers University Press, 1993).
20. Becker, *Outsiders*, 148.
21. Peter Berger, *The Sacred Canopy: Elements of a Sociological Theory of Religion* (New York: Doubleday, 1969), 33.
22. Rodney Stark and Roger Finke, *Acts of Faith: Explaining the Human Side of Religion* (Berkeley, CA: University of California Press, 2000).
23. The term "active" has a specific meaning among Mormons. An "active" Mormon is one who attends church frequently, participates in Mormon church rituals, and professes high levels of belief in Mormon doctrine.
24. Norman K. Denzin, *The Research Act: A Theoretical Introduction to Sociological Methods* (Englewood Cliffs, NJ: Prentice Hall, 1989).
25. George A. Theodorson and Achilles G. Theodorson, *A Modern Dictionary of Sociology* (New York: Barnes and Noble, 1969), 460; *cf.* H. H. Gerth and C. Wright Mills (eds), *From Max Weber: Essays in Sociology* (New York: Oxford University Press, 1947).

CHAPTER TWO
Mormon Theology and Homosexuality

Restrictions on the expression of sexuality espoused by conservative Christian churches in the United States find their provenance in the venerable Law of Moses, a comprehensive code of conduct for the ancient Hebrew people. The law, as outlined in the book of Leviticus, prohibits various sexual practices such as rape, adultery, bestiality, incest, and others.[1] Not the least among these injunctions is one widely interpreted as a prohibition against male homosexuality. Male homosexual relations are called an "abomination" by God, and according to the law, are a capital offense. Indeed, God warns the Hebrews that: "If a man ... lie with mankind, as he lieth with a woman, both of them have committed an abomination: they shall surely be put to death; their blood shall be upon them."[2]

The notion of male homosexuality as sin is based in part on the Christian scriptures as well. Although references to male homosexual behavior in the New Testament are infrequent, the passages that do exist denounce the practice. For example, the apostle Paul, writing to the church at Corinth, explicitly states that homosexuals and the "effeminate" will not be allowed into the kingdom of God.[3]

In addition to a belief that male homosexuality is inherently sinful, many Christian churches are intolerant of gay relationships because of their conviction that homosexuality is to society what cancer is to the body—left unchecked it will grow, spread, and mutate. Homosexuality must be eradicated and not just eschewed because the presence of homosexuality is indicative of cultural degeneration and moral decay.[4] This belief is rooted in the story of the cities of Sodom and Gomorrah found in the 19th chapter of Genesis. These cities—which serve as the archetype of a sinful society—were annihilated by God because of their licentiousness. The apostle Paul, writing to the fledgling Christian church in Rome, is believed by many Christians pastors to have identified male homosexuality as the principle sin of Sodom and Gomorrah, and the primary reason why God chose to utterly destroy the cities:

> Wherefore God also gave them up to uncleanness through the lusts of their own hearts, to dishonor their own bodies between themselves ... For this cause God gave them up unto vile affections: for even their women did change the natural use into that which is against nature: And likewise also the men, leaving the natural use of the woman, burned in their lust one toward another; men with men working that which is unseemly, and receiving in themselves that recompense of their error which was meet.[5]

While the traditional interpretation of these Bible verses is contested,[6] these texts, and several others like them, have been used throughout history by clergy and exegetes to legitimize the Christian attitude toward homosexual behavior.

Homosexuality and American Christianity

Christian attitudes like those presented above, though centuries old and firmly entrenched, have come under heavy fire. Heartened by the strides toward equality made by African Americans and women in the 1960s, participants in the developing gay rights movement began to lobby against institutionalized homophobia in the churches. For the first time in America, many gay church goers were beginning to emerge from the closet to demand acceptance both for themselves and their lifestyle from the Christian churches.

Support for their cause has been slow and modest, but some advances have been made. The birth and growth of the nationally prominent Metropolitan Community Church, which openly embraces gay members, is but one of the many Christian groups which has emerged to pastor the large Christian gay community. In 1972, the United Methodist Church accepted a declaration that "extend[ed] to all persons, including those of homosexual orientation, the redemptive life of the church community."[7]

The highly publicized case of the Episcopal Bishop of Newark, the Right Reverend John Shelby Spong, is typical of the type of change that was beginning to occur within mainline Protestant churches by the late 1980s. In 1988, Spong began to openly advocate the admission and ordination of gays and lesbians to the Episcopal clergy—a policy that ultimately led to the ordination of a gay bishop in 2003.[8] Spong's crusade is still ahead of its time for most of American Christianity, but changes like these have prompted many sociologists of religion to admit that attitudes toward homosexuality are softening, and that gay people are moving into the mainstream of some mainline Protestant denominations.

Nevertheless, homophobia is still abundant in American society, and many traditional and conservative churches are resisting the tide of tolerance that is slowly rising over the traditional prohibitions of mainline Protestantism. The fundamentalist revitalization of the 1980s, fueled in part by the AIDS scare, brought with it a renewed and vigorous attack on homosexuals from the Christian right. Claiming to go "back to the Bible," and subscribing to the doctrines of Biblical infallibility and the universal applicability and literal interpretation of scripture, members of these churches are strident and vociferous in their denunciation of homosexuals.

Today, conservative religious groups are the front-line soldiers in the fight against gay rights and legislation protecting gay people, and the rhetoric from this camp remains as caustic as ever. Thus, in spite of the modest gains discussed above, it is still safe to assert that a majority of Christian churches in the U.S. still consider homosexuality to be deviant behavior.

Mormonism and Homosexuality

One religious organization that has given very little ground in its rejection of homosexuality is the Church of Jesus Christ of Latter-day Saints, commonly called the Mormon, or LDS church. Since the church was founded in 1830, Mormon church leaders have been relatively silent on the issue of homosexuality. Discussions of the subject appear very infrequently in the speeches of Mormon leaders throughout the 19th and first half of the 20th centuries. However, since the gay rights movement emerged from the closet in the late 1960s, Mormon apostles and prophets[9] have begun an infrequent, but unequivocal denunciation of homosexuality in official church printed matter and from the pulpit. Since the Stonewall riots of 1969, which vaulted the nascent gay rights movement to national prominence, LDS clergymen have condemned gay people and their lifestyle in no uncertain terms, calling homosexual behavior a "sexual perversion" and an "abuse of the sacred power to create [life]."[10] From about 1970 to the present, homosexuality is mentioned with increasing frequency in the church's semi-annual general conferences, and in every case it is condemned with the strongest of language.

Individual apostles have compared the seriousness of homosexuality with murder, and have implied that the acceptance of homosexuality was the reason for the downfall not only Sodom and Gomorrah, but of the empires of Greece and Rome as well.[11] Spencer W. Kimball, twelfth prophet of the church, called homosexuality "repugnant," "wretched wickedness," "degenerate," "unnatural," and "ugliness" in a book that is a bestseller in Mormon bookstores.[12] And apostle Bruce R. McConkie stated that because "homosexual abominations are fast becoming the norm of life among the wicked and ungodly," the world will soon be as evil as it was in the days of Noah.[13]

Research shows that the words of these leaders have not fallen on deaf ears. Mormons are among the most intolerant of American religious groups with regard to accepting gay people and their lifestyle. Glenn Vernon found that when rating the sinfulness of various practices such as lying or theft on a scale of 1 to 10, a full 92 percent of Mormon college students rate homosexuality as a 10, or "extremely wrong"—only adultery and murder fared worse.[14] When Wilford E. Smith asked a similar sample to rank a list of sins according to their seriousness, homosexuality was ranked number one, regardless of the respondent's gender, and regardless of whether or not the respondent attended church frequently or infrequently.[15]

Nevertheless, there are members of the Church of Jesus Christ of Latter-day Saints who are gay. And, not surprisingly, these pronouncements have become a vexing problem for these believers. As they see gay people in the larger society push for acceptance and anti-discrimination legislation, gay Mormons are faced with the knowledge that their church simply does not see rights for gay people as a credible cause. As they see the emergence of tolerance in mainline denominations and the rise of Protestant organizations specifically geared to meet the spiritual needs of gay Christians, they are faced with the precariousness of their spiritual plight.

Of course, difficulty harmonizing a homosexual orientation with one's religion is not unique to Mormons. Thumma's ethnography of a gay Evangelical group shows that most of those coming to the group were in the midst of an "identity crisis."[16] Thumma cites two new members who were forced to confront this crisis:

> 'I will not and cannot disregard my faith (nor my sexual orientation). I often find myself compromising my beliefs. The Lord is disappointed with me.' Another writer stated, 'I have abstained from sexual involvement with others for three years because of my fear of breaking God's law. I miss the close fellowship of a lover, but I'm scared that I will go to hell if I do. I'm so lonely.'[17]

Thumma notes that while most gay Evangelicals came to the group embroiled in identity conflict, the fellowship of other gay Christians was successful in assuaging the mental anguish associated with the dissonance. Thus, while their conflict was a difficult ordeal, by changing congregations (or, at most, Christian denominations), they were able to find a body of believers that met their spiritual needs by accepting them as homosexuals *and* Christians.

Mormon Doctrine and Homosexuality

This route is not as easily taken by gay Mormons. Unlike most Protestant churches in the United States, Mormons believe that there is no true salvation outside the Mormon church. Moreover, the doctrine of the LDS church is fundamentally different from traditional Protestant teachings, and most believing Mormon homosexuals would find themselves on unfamiliar turf should they seek succor from an accepting Protestant sect.[18]

To exacerbate this problem, one of the key tenets of the LDS church is that the original, true gospel of Jesus Christ was corrupted and twisted by Roman Catholicism and Protestant reformers. Because of this, God's priesthood, which according to Mormonism is the power to act in His name, was taken from the earth. The founder of Mormonism, Joseph Smith, claimed to have restored this lost power to the earth in a vision in 1829. Thus, for members of the LDS church, only baptisms, ordinations, and other ceremonies performed under the auspices of priesthood power (i.e., performed in the Mormon church) are recognized by God. So, while a gay Christian can find salvation in another, more tolerant church, Mormons believe that theirs is the only true church—no other alternative religious group is sanctioned by God.[19] The *Book of Mormon* states:

> There are save two churches only; the one is the church of the Lamb of God, and the other is the church of the devil; wherefore, whoso belongeth not to the church of the Lamb of God belongeth to that great church, which is the mother of abominations; and she is the whore of all the earth.[20]

While it is true that such caustic denunciations of other churches have been tamed in the speeches of Mormon authorities over the last two decades, the church still holds essentially the same view of other religions that it has held from the beginning. As Tanner and Tanner observe: "present-day leaders of the Mormon church are becoming more subtle in their attacks on other churches, [but] they still teach that the Mormon church is the only true church and that all others are in a state of apostasy."[21] Thus, it is easy to see that gay Mormons are in a peculiar predicament. They can neither find solace in their own religion, nor can they easily seek to meet their spiritual needs in another sect.

There are still other factors that marginalize gay members of the LDS church. Commitment to Mormonism is heightened for members by the emphasis the church places on individual religious experiences. Such experiences are defined by Mormon leaders as sure evidence that the LDS church is the true faith. These religious experiences are highly significant for Mormons, and are continually reaffirmed and recounted in monthly congregational meetings where members disclose to one another their strong belief, or "testimony" that theirs is the only true church. Youth in the church are encouraged to "gain a testimony" through a regimen of fasting, prayer, and adherence to the commandments. The practice of seeking a supernatural encounter is modeled after the experience of Joseph Smith, who, upon praying to God to ask which of all the Christian sects was true, received a vision of God and Jesus Christ. Members are also told to ask God about the truthfulness of the *Book of Mormon*, and in the final chapter of that book, readers are admonished upon reading the work to:

> ... ask God the Eternal Father, in the name of Christ, if these things are not true; and if ye shall ask with a sincere heart, with real intent, having faith in Christ, he will manifest the truth of it unto you, by the power of the Holy Ghost.[22]

The "manifestation" that follows this prayer has an indelible effect on those who have had it. Most describe a "burning in the bosom" or a warm feeling telling them that the book is true. Often this experience is an emotional one, and Mormons recounting it for others often become tearful in the telling. Not every church member who reads and prays about the *Book of Mormon* reports such an experience, but the occurrence is common in the church, and for those who have had it, it is often life-altering. One gay Mormon stated:

> I can't deny my testimony. I know the church is true like I know I'm standing here. I know that the *Book of Mormon* is true with all my heart. Nothing can convince me that this is not the gospel of Jesus Christ. But I also know that I am gay. I don't know what to do about that. I don't know what I *can* do about that.

Finally, Mormons also have unique beliefs about the nature and function of marriage that set them apart from other Christians. According to the LDS faith, there are two kinds of marriage. "Temporal" marriages are those marriages which are performed by the power of the state, or by clergy from other faiths. These marriages, the church teaches, are legally binding, and the expression of sexuality within them is appropriate and expected. However, temporal marriages are, as the words of the familiar ceremony suggest, "'til death do us part."

Eternal marriage, the preferred counterpart to temporal marriage, is not only legally recognized by the state, but is also sanctioned by God. Eternal marriage can only be performed by the power of the Mormon priesthood, and can only be transacted in special temples set aside for this purpose. According to Mormon belief, eternal marriage, or "temple marriage," creates a union between husband and wife that remains effectual not only in this world, but in the hereafter as well. Entrance into the temple, where such marriages are performed, is strictly limited to members of the church who are screened by their bishops and stake presidents[23] to ensure their orthodoxy.

But such marriages are more than just eternal relationships. According to LDS theology, being married is essential for complete salvation. Church doctrine states that temple marriage is a *sine-qua-non* for entrance into the highest degree of heaven—a place where people are allowed to become gods and create worlds of their own, in much the same capacity as the Creator of this earth.[24] This process of world building involves creating "spirit children" who will inhabit these worlds, and thus marriage is necessary for the inhabitants of this "celestial kingdom." The doctrine of marriage and its centrality to Mormon theology was spelled out by Joseph Smith in 1843. The prophet wrote:

> Therefore, if a man marry him a wife in the world, and he marry her not by me nor by my word, and he covenant with her so long as he is in the world and she with him, their covenant and marriage are not of force when they are dead. ... Therefore, when they are out of the world they neither marry nor are given in marriage; but are appointed angels in heaven, which angels are ministering servants, to minister for those who are worthy of a far more, and an exceeding, and an eternal weight of glory. For these angels did not abide by my law; therefore they cannot be enlarged, but remain separately and singly, without exaltation.[25]

Writing of those who are married for "time and all eternity," the prophet revealed that, should they remain faithful, "Then shall they be gods, because they have no end; therefore shall they be from everlasting to everlasting ... they [shall] be gods, because they have all power, and the angels are subject unto them."[26]

Thus, those who are faithful but do not have the benefit of temple marriage will act as the servants of those who do. Only heterosexual marriages are performed in the temple, and great emphasis is placed on marriage in the LDS church. Single men and women, as they approach their later twenties, experience increasing pressure from family and church leaders to find a spouse and continue their push toward exaltation.[27]

This view of marriage, more than anything else, seems to marginalize gay members of the church, and many have resigned themselves to a lesser degree of glory in Mormon heaven. One exchange between this researcher and a gay college student, recently returned from an LDS mission,[28] typifies the depth of this resignation:

RESEARCHER: So then, what about eternal progression?[29]
INFORMANT: What about it?
RESEARCHER: Well, how do you see yourself fitting in?
INFORMANT: Well, the *D & C*[30] says that we'll be ministering angels if we aren't married, but I think that will be okay, you know, I'll be a ministering angel. I think that is kind of what the Holy Ghost does, you know, kind of a messenger for the gods type of thing.
RESEARCHER: So maybe you can't be like God the Father, but you can be like the Holy Ghost?
INFORMANT: Yeah. Something like that.
RESEARCHER: So do you think that the Holy Ghost might be gay?
INFORMANT: No.

Mormon marriages are also expected to be fruitful, not just in the afterlife, but on this earth as well. Large families are idealized in the church, and having many children is seen as a badge of orthodoxy and faithfulness.[31] Mormon women are encouraged to drop out of the labor force when they get married so that their presence in the home can facilitate the care of a large family.[32] The use of artificial birth control is discouraged, and having an abortion is an excommunicable offense.[33]

The Mormon preference for large families is predicated on the belief that people live as spirits in heaven before they take on a body and come to earth. Obtaining a body is necessary for exaltation, and so it behooves Mormon couples to provide the opportunity to come to earth for as many of God's spirit children as possible As one observer, writing in the letters to the editor section of a Mormon literary journal remarked: "The infertility of homosexual relationships strikes at the very heart of Mormon sexual ethics."[34] The Mormon apostle, and later church president, Spencer W. Kimball epitomized these sentiments when he wrote:

> Of the adverse social effects of homosexuality, none is more significant than the effect on marriage and home. The normal, God-given sexual relationship is the procreative act between man and woman in honorable marriage. ... In this context, where stands the perversion of homosexuality? ... If the abominable practice became universal it would depopulate the earth in a single generation. It would nullify God's great program for his spirit children in that it would leave countless unem-

> bodied spirits in the heavenly world without the chance for the opportunities of mortality.[35]

In sum, it would seem that Mormonism places overwhelming theological hurdles in the path of its homosexual members, while at the same time stressing personal religious experiences which make it very hard for them to apostatize. One gay Mormon sums it up thusly:

> I feel great pain that the church I love so much and have devoted my life to offers me only no-win options. If I remain single, I will be discriminated against, as positions of significant responsibility and leadership are filled by married men. I will be hounded relentlessly to get married, and—according to Mormon myth—I will be denied exaltation and condemned to spend eternity serving my married brothers as a ministering angel, whatever that is. If I marry, I run the risk of making myself and at least one other person miserable for many years, with the almost certain risk of divorce. I also have the option of living with a male companion and either leaving the church because of guilt, or being forced out by excommunication. At the moment, I am having difficulty deciding which of these options I want most.[36]

Another writer recognizes this theological quagmire and admits that leaving the church is much harder than it may appear:

> Having been raised a Mormon, it is impossible to ever separate oneself emotionally from the church. For many, it remains an irresolvable antagonism in their lives. My non-Mormon homosexual friends have often observed that breaking from their hostile church was one of the more positive things they had done, but the Mormon homosexuals they have known remain inextricably tangled with the church. When they realize the extreme position the church takes, they are incredulous that I would continue to be active. Their religious background does not give them adequate perspective of the profound effect which being raised a Mormon has on the lives of its members. ... Being a Mormon and homosexual brings the dilemma into even sharper focus. The "shadow of the creed" with its strong family tradition, sexual purity, and doctrine of celestial marriage is indelibly impressed upon the young man's character. Few religions and even cultures value and practice fellowship to the degree experienced by Mormons. It is commonly observed that being Mormon is a complete way of life.[37]

Because of this "complete way of life," it is not uncommon for gay Mormons, at one time or another, to seek help from ecclesiastical leaders, hoping for understanding and assistance in coming to grips with the contradictions inherent in the incongruous interplay of sexual orientation and LDS religious belief. For this reason, the church has been forced to develop institutionalized policies for bishops and stake presidents for dealing with those who come to their leaders confessing what the church calls "homosexual problems." We turn to these in the next chapter.

Notes

1. See Leviticus chapters 18–20. Unless otherwise indicated, all quotations from the Bible are from the King James Version.
2. See Leviticus 18:22 and 20:13.
3. First Corinthians 6:9. Two Greek words are used to convey Paul's feelings about male homosexuality in these verses. The first, μαλακοι (pronounced *malakoi*) connotes softness, passivity and femininity. The second, αρσενοκοιται (pronounced *arsenokoitai*) is a vulgar term and literally means, as is evident from the etymology, "one who engages in anal sex." See F. F. Bruce, *I and II Corinthians* (Grand Rapids, MI: Eerdmans, 1971). Bruce and other commentators note that the words used together refer to both the "passive" and "active" role in male homosexual intercourse.
4. Erling Jorstad, *Holding Fast; Pressing On: Religion in America in the 1980s* (New York: Praeger, 1990).
5. Romans 1:24, 26–27.
6. For a conservative interpretation of these verses see Robert A. J. Gagnon, *The Bible and Homosexual Practice: Texts and Hermeneutics* (Nashville, TN: Abingdon Press, 2002). For a response to these arguments, see Robin Scroggs, *New Testament and Homosexuality* (Minneapolis, MN: Fortress Press, 1984).
7. Leo Rosten, *Religions of America: Ferment and Faith in an Age of Crisis* (New York: Simon and Schuster, 1975), 541.
8. John Shelby Spong, *Living in Sin? A Bishop Rethinks Sexuality* (San Francisco: Harper and Row, 1988).
9. The Church of Jesus Christ of Latter-day Saints is governed by a body of clergymen known as the General Authorities. Of these authorities, the apostles and the living prophet are the highest in authority and power. Typically, there are 12 apostles, modeled after the organization of Jesus's ministry.
10. *Ensign* November 1982, 4. *Ensign*, November 1986, 46.
11. *Ensign*, May 1980, 6. *Ensign*, November 1977, 73.
12. Spencer W. Kimball, *The Miracle of Forgiveness* (Salt Lake City: Bookcraft, 1969).
13. *Ensign*, November 1980, 50.

14. Glenn M. Vernon, *Mormonism: A Sociological Perspective*. (Salt Lake City: *n. p.*, 1980).
15. Wilford E. Smith, "Mormon Sex Standards on College Campuses, or Deal Us Out of the Sexual Revolution," *Dialogue: A Journal of Mormon Thought* 10, no. 2 (1977): 76–81.
16. Thumma, "Negotiating a Religious Identity," *Sociological Analysis* 52, no. 4 (1991): 333–347.
17. Ibid., 338.
18. For instance, Mormons believe that God has a body of flesh and bone, while Protestants believe that God is spirit. Mormons do not accept the doctrine of the trinity, while it is a pillar of Protestantism. Mormons also believe in the *Book of Mormon*, a volume of scripture unique to Mormonism and its offshoots.
19. All matters of Mormon doctrine and practice in this chapter (and throughout this book) are discussed at length in Bruce R. McKonkie *Mormon Doctrine* (Salt Lake City: Bookcraft, 1966). McKonkie's work is arranged in encyclopedic form, and it serves as an excellent resource for those wishing to understand Mormon theology. See also Coke Newell, *Latter Days: A Guided Tour through Six Billion Years of Mormonism* (New York: Saint Martin's Press, 2000), and Robert L. Millet, *The Mormon Faith: A New Look at Christianity* (Salt Lake City: Shadow Mountain, 1998).
20. I Nephi 14:10.
21. Jerald Tanner and Sandra Tanner, *Mormonism: Shadow or Reality¿* (Salt Lake City: Modern Microfilm, 1987), 3.
22. Moroni 10:4.
23. Mormon congregations, or "wards" are led by a bishop, whereas "stakes," which are conglomerates of 7 to 12 wards roughly equivalent in scope to Catholic dioceses, are headed by stake presidents. Bishops and stake presidents (and virtually all other local leaders within the church) are lay volunteers who serve without pay.
24. The Mormon concept of heaven is very different from that of other Christian denominations. Within Mormonism, heaven is comprised of three distinct "degrees of glory." It is only in the highest of these three heavens, called the "celestial kingdom," that men and woman can achieve a fullness of glory, or "exhalation."
25. *Doctrine and Covenants* 132:15–16.
26. *Doctrine and Covenants* 132:20.
27. Marybeth Raynes and Erin Parsons, "Single Cursedness: An Overview of LDS Authorities Statements about Unmarried People," *Dialogue: A Journal of Mormon Thought* 16, no. 3 (1983): 35–45.
28. At the age of nineteen, all young Mormon men are enjoined to serve a two year proselytizing mission for the church. The purpose of this mission is to seek and convert people to Mormonism.
29. Mormons refer to the process of achieving salvation and exhalation in the celestial kingdom as "eternal progression."

30. "*D & C*" is a colloquial term for *Doctrine and Covenants*, a book of Mormon scripture.
31. Tim B. Heaton, "Four Characteristics of the Mormon Family: Contemporary Research on Chastity, Conjugality, Children and Chauvinism," *Dialogue: A Journal of Mormon Thought* 20, no. 2 (1987): 101–114.
32. Marylin Warenski, *Patriarchs and Politics: The Plight of the Mormon Woman* (New York: McGraw-Hill, 1980).
33. McKonkie, *Mormon Doctrine* 85–86.
34. Paul Emile Le Blanc, "A Question of Love," *Dialogue: A Journal of Mormon Thought* 20, no. 1 (1987): 10.
35. Kimball, *The Miracle of Forgiveness*, 80–81.
36. [Name Withheld], "Choking in the Dust," *Dialogue: A Journal of Mormon Thought* 23, no. 4 (1990): 5.
37. Cloy Jenkins, *Prologue: An Examination of Mormon Attitudes Towards Homosexuality* (Provo, UT: Prometheus Enterprises, 1978), 47.

CHAPTER THREE
LDS Church Policy and Homosexuality

Until the last half of the twentieth century, LDS church leaders saw no need to directly address the issue of homosexuality. Only when the first rumblings of what was to become the gay rights movement began to challenge traditional assumptions about sexual orientation did the church begin to respond with policies, actions, and rhetoric directed toward both gay people in the church and the issue of gay rights in the larger society.

The church's first efforts to deal with the issue began in 1959 when Mormon apostles Mark E. Petersen and Spencer W. Kimball were placed in charge of developing and administering policy on sexual matters for church members. Regarding homosexuality, the substance of the policy was clear: those who had engaged in homosexual behavior were almost always excommunicated; those who had not had homosexual encounters but were nevertheless inclined to do so were prescribed a regimen of prayer and fasting and were given an opportunity to allow God to change them through faith and obedience. Those who were not "changed" were likewise cut off from the fellowship of the church.[1]

A decade later, apostle Kimball published his work, *The Miracle of Forgiveness*, a well-known and frequently cited Mormon classic that deals extensively with the subject of sexual immorality. Schow, Schow, and Raynes note that by the time this work was published, Kimball "had formulated ideas about homosexuality which have dominated church policy since that time."[2]

Kimball's disdain for homosexuality is clear. In a chapter called "Crime Against Nature," Kimball calls homosexuality "an ugly sin, repugnant to those who find no temptation in it."[3] Throughout, it is taken for granted that homosexuality is a matter of personal choice, a sinful practice, and one that can be cured. He writes:

> After consideration of the evil aspects, the ugliness and prevalence of the evil of homosexuality, the glorious thing to remember is that it is curable and forgivable. ... Certainly it can be overcome, for there are numerous happy people who were once involved in its clutches and who have since completely transformed their lives. Therefore to those who say that this practice or any other evil is incurable, I respond: "How can you say the door cannot be opened until your knuckles are bloody, till your head is bruised, till your muscles are sore? It can be done."[4]

Kimball states that homosexuality is a level of perversion reached only after one has indulged in "gateway" sexual sins. Early in the chapter he identifies masturbation as a cause of homosexuality. In turn, homosexuality can serve as a gateway to even more grievous sexual sin. The apostle writes:

> Sin in sex practices tends to have a "snowballing" effect. As the restraints fall away, Satan incites the carnal man to ever-deepening degeneracy in his search for excitement until in many instances he is lost to any former considerations of decency. Thus it is that through the ages, perhaps as an extension of homosexual practices, men and women have sunk even to seeking sexual satisfactions with animals.[5]

The Miracle of Forgiveness solidified and codified the church's position on homosexuality: that it is sin, it is chosen behavior, and it can be changed. When the church developed a handbook for bishops on how to counsel gay members, Kimball's ideas served as the foundation. Entitled simply *Homosexuality,* the handbook states that homosexual behavior is unacceptable to the Lord because it defiles the sacred power of procreation, stains the lives of those involved with sin, and may be linked to crime and abuse.[6] But it goes beyond Kimball's views by declaring that homosexual *thoughts* and *fantasies* are sinful, whether or not they are accompanied by overt sexual acts.[7] It further states that the development of homosexuality is associated with a disturbed family background, poor relationships with peers, a domineering mother, a passive father, and masturbation.[8]

The handbook's central theme is that homosexuality is freely chosen. This claim rests on the Mormon belief that humans existed in a pristine state with God before coming to earth.[9] Life on this planet, the church teaches, is a test to determine who can remain faithful and return to God's presence. All people are free to choose whether they will keep the commandments or reject them, and hence everyone is responsible for their own salvation. It is heretical to believe that anyone could be born with ineluctable desires that might compromise their ability to make correct choices.[10] No one is foreordained to evil, or tempted beyond their capacity to resist,[11] and thus homosexuality cannot be rooted in biology.

Changing the sexual orientation of gay Latter-day Saints is the explicit purpose of this handbook. It instructs bishops that inspired prophets have made assurances that homosexuality can be changed, and that they should communicate this idea to those who come to them for counseling. The regimen of change involves fasting and prayer, using church leaders as role models, and appropriate contact with the opposite sex. It also entails refraining from masturbation, and eliminating this practice is cited as a prerequisite to reorienting homosexual desires. Those who are unable or unwilling to change face excommunication. The booklet closes with moving testimonials from those who have supposedly changed through this method.[12]

Gay men are admonished to start heterosexual dating, and to steadily increase its frequency, even if they must force themselves.[13] Marriage is the implied resolution of this dating, and many gay Mormon men report that they were strongly urged to marry by bishops and other church leaders. The tacit assumption behind these urgings is that once a person begins a heterosexual relationship in earnest, nature will take over. The consequences of this policy, as we shall see, were disastrous.

Homosexuality and the Mormon Mental Health Community

To further assist gay Mormons in changing their sexual orientation, the church also enlisted the help of LDS psychologists and mental health clinicians. Long after the American Psychiatric Association's

1974 action removing homosexuality from the DSM-IIIR, church-owned Brigham Young University developed "aversion therapy" programs using electric shock as negative reinforcement in an attempt to alter and suppress homosexual thoughts and feelings. Subjects in these studies were shown pictures of men in sexual poses and were delivered painful electric shocks if these pictures produced sexual arousal.[14] At least one Ph.D. dissertation was written based on these studies.[15]

Those who claim to have successfully changed their sexual orientation through prayer and fasting, heterosexual dating, or "aversion therapy" are few and far between. Furthermore, the failure of these programs has not been from lack of trying on the part of those involved. Indeed, one LDS bishop remarked:

> My own anecdotal experience is that not only would most Latter-day Saint homosexuals change their orientation if they could; but many, perhaps most, have tried desperately, sometimes over a sustained period of years, to do exactly that. ... In my experience, homosexuality is one of the major problems facing the church today.[16]

Realizing the depth of this "major problem," a new battery of Mormon mental health professionals gradually began to speak out in LDS journals and conferences, pushing the church for a new stance on homosexuality—a realistic stance that did not demand a change in sexual orientation. One such authority was Carlford Broderick, former director of the marriage and family therapy program at the University of Southern California. In a book published by church-owned Deseret Book Company, Broderick admits that homosexual orientation can only be redirected toward heterosexuality through "a series of miracles."[17]

Victor L. Brown Jr., a Mormon psychologist, states that while change is and ought to be the goal of gay Mormons, a new definition of "change" needs to be emphasized. Brown states that while one cannot change orientation, one can realize "a kind, humane, overall enjoyment of warmth and affection with both men and women, without erotic undertones."[18] Lastly, LDS psychiatrist Jan Stout, writing in a popular journal for Mormon scholarship, states flatly that he does not believe that homosexuality is chosen. He also notes that rather than seeing success among gay Mormons seeking change, "[His] clinical experience has indicated that the majority of Mormon homosexuals eventually drift away from their faith, live tenuously in the closet, or react with angry disillusionment."[19]

Not surprisingly, many gay Mormons, apprised of the words of these clinicians, and emotionally brutalized by their encounters with bishops and stake presidents, became disgruntled with the Mormon church's brand of therapy. As a result, many began to talk about taking matters into their own hands. One homosexual church member writes:

> At present, to be Mormon and homosexual requires considerable compromise of either self identity or religious principles, this ever-present dichotomy creates inevitable conflicts. The extent to which the Latter-day Saint belief system is accepted or tolerated by Mormon homosexuals is ultimately their own decision. However, if Mormon gays and lesbians are ever to gain greater control over their lives, they must do so by empowering themselves. ... No longer powerless, the new Mormon gay and lesbian—those who have taken the charge to shepherd their own destinies—have begun to establish a base for change in public opinion within the church.[20]

This notion of empowerment became the driving force behind a new move afoot by gay Mormons to press the LDS church for acceptance. At the risk—and often expense—of their church membership, some gay Mormons began to emerge from the closet and to look within their own community for help in resolving the contradictions between their sexual preference and spiritual needs.

The Gay Rights Movement within Mormonism

Since 1978, gay Mormons have formed organizations and support groups to help ease the stress associated with being gay and LDS. The most ambitious and successful of these efforts is Affirmation, an independent organization formed in early 1978 by gay and lesbian Mormons to specifically address the spiritual and psychological needs of those trying to harmonize the doctrines of the church with homosexuality. Affirmation is organized into regional chapters which meet monthly to discuss relevant issues and provide opportunities for gay Mormons to meet one another. The group also publishes a monthly newsletter. Affirmation's charter asserts that "homosexuality and homosexual relations can be consistent with and supported by the gospel of Jesus Christ."[21] The charter further states that the purpose of Affirmation is to "work for the understanding and acceptance of gays and lesbians as full, equal and worthy persons within the Church of Jesus Christ of Latter-day Saints," and to "provide support for people experiencing difficulty reconciling their sexual orientation with traditional Mormon beliefs .... "[22]

Despite the explicit statement of purpose contained in the charter, individual members of Affirmation range in opinion from those wanting assistance and support in their attempt to change their sexual orientation or live celibate lives, to those who believe that gay people should be given the right to marry in Mormon temples. A significant number of Affirmation members also openly denounce the LDS leadership, claiming that the church, once true, has fallen into apostasy. Evidence for this apostasy is the church's institutionalized homophobia—something, they reason, that God would never countenance. Those who fall into this category have typically requested excommunication (a request the church immediately honors), but nevertheless profess to have "testimonies" of the *Book of Mormon* and the divine mission of Joseph Smith. Most say that they would return to the fellowship of the church if homosexual relationships were officially countenanced.

Some of those in this camp attempted to form their own church in 1985. On August 28 of that year, Antonio Feliz, a former Mormon bishop, organized The Restoration Church of Jesus Christ. This tiny schism accepts the *Book of Mormon*, the divine mission of Joseph Smith, and temple marriage, but differs from the LDS church in that its constituency is almost exclusively gay. Feliz's church began to actively proselytize among the gay community, and became known among those familiar with it as "the gay Mormon church."[23]

Other attempts have been made to meet the spiritual needs of gay Mormons as well. For example, there is a gay BYU alumni association. The presence of gay students at BYU is particularly troublesome for the church, since, as one observer put it, "For many Mormons BYU is their city on a hill and the very juxtaposition of 'gay' and 'BYU' ... is an uncomfortable reality."[24] Nevertheless, this researcher was invited to visit and interview members of the gay underground at BYU, and discovered that at least one organized support group exists to help those at the university cope.

Other organizations include HELP (Homosexual Education for Latter-day Saint Parents), a support group for the parents of gay Mormons, and a gay returned missionary association. A publication designed to meet the needs of gay and lesbian Mormons, dubbed *New Horizons,* launched its premier issue in 1991, and the Gay and Lesbian Alliance (GLA) on the campuses of Utah State University and the University of Utah have many Latter-day Saints within their ranks.

Other groups exist, and several more have come and gone over the past decade. Most, however, have been short-lived and insignificant. Only Affirmation, discussed at length in chapter six, has been able to persist in any meaningful way. The chief reason why most of these groups are unable to attract a significant following or retain their members stems from the unique theology and structure of the Mormon church. Harmonizing Mormonism and homosexuality is not an easy task, and it is little wonder why most such groups are unable to do it.

When asked about the numerous support groups for gay and lesbian Mormons that have come and gone over the years, one counselor at a Utah LDS Social Services center with an MSW from Brigham Young University expressed these sentiments:

> **INFORMANT:** It seems like every week a new organization for gay or lesbian Mormons emerges. They spring up, talk about what the church needs to do, print up a newsletter, and then fizzle out. They're never around for more than a few months.
> **RESEARCHER:** Why do you suppose they fizzle out?
> **INFORMANT:** Why do you suppose?
> **RESEARCHER:** I'm asking you.
> **INFORMANT:** Because—and I'm not going to mince words here—they are kicking against the pricks.[25] They're not happy. They need to realize that wickedness never was happiness[26] and get with the program. They don't need a lot of organizations and support groups telling them how to reconcile being gay and being LDS. They need to stop being lazy, get down on their knees, and repent.

Regardless of the reasons for the instability of most of these organizations, the fact remains that the vast majority of gay Mormons do not seek them out for help and support. Indeed, in a church with over 12 million members, there must be hundreds of thousands of homosexual Saints—far more than in all of the organizations designed to pastor them combined.

Nevertheless, despite their small numbers, an increasingly vocal and organized gay minority began to stir the church to action in the 1980s. Embarrassed by public knowledge of its failed programs for turning gay people straight, the church began to open its eyes and ears to the concerns of many Mormon social workers and the gay people burdened under the yoke of church policies. Church leaders sought out the professionals at LDS Social Services, a department within the church staffed by temple worthy Mormons trained in the behavioral sciences, for insights on how to deal with gay members. (The church had earlier turned such things as serious marital problems and emotional and mental disorders away from local bishops and over to social services.)[27] The result of this shift in administrative strategy was a substantial change in the way the church deals with homosexuality. Most of the informants for this study who have been active in the church for some time report that the church has, in recent years, become more realistic in helping gay members cope with their problems.

Today, gay Mormons who make an earnest effort to live within the church's guidelines are rarely excommunicated. Some of the informants for this study have been in ongoing counseling with their ecclesiastical leaders and LDS social workers for periods of three or more years, and despite frequent "slip-ups," have managed to keep their church membership more or less intact. Ordinarily, only those gay members who are defiant, unrepentant, or who specifically ask to have their names expunged from church records are in real danger of excommunication. Most informants in this study report that those who appear penitent before their bishops and stake presidents will almost always be given another chance to repent, provided these appearances happen with decreasing frequency. There are exceptions to this general rule, however.

More importantly than not removing gay members from its rolls, the church has also looked the other way at efforts to counsel and pastor gay members by certain bishops and other church leaders. The most ambitious attempt to meet the spiritual needs of gay Mormons from within the church was administered by bishop Stan Roberts, who served as bishop of the San Francisco single adult ward from 1984 to 1989. When Roberts, a retired businessman, assumed his calling in 1984, he was amazed to discover that over 20 percent of his male parishioners were gay.[28] Roberts, faced with the collapse of his congregation, reasoned that *being* homosexual was not a sin, but that homosexual *behavior* was. He concluded that as long as gay members of his ward abstained from sexual activity, they could not only attend church without fear of excommunication, but could hold the priesthood and certain positions in the lay clergy as well.[29] When asked if he ever condoned homosexual behavior or knowingly allowed sexually active gay men to receive priesthood callings, Roberts responded:

> Not to my knowledge. Of course, I could have been deceived. But I got to know them fairly well. If somebody had a lover or they were sleeping with somebody I didn't give them a calling. I think in the eyes of the church anybody who says that they are homosexual is an "active" homosexual—sexually—but that's not the case. ... I've had a lot of gays ask me if they could move their membership to the ward, meaning, "Will you allow me to have my lover?" I replied that it's not a matter of me allowing you to do anything. I'm an administrator in the gospel, and these are my perimeters. ... I can't change the commandments and I still have to go by the handbook. I need to be tempered by the Spirit, but I have never been willing to say, "It's all right if you have that kind of relationship."[30]

Still, even for those who were openly involved in gay relationships, Roberts did not convene church courts, although he regarded such behavior as unacceptable. Roberts notes:

> If people were blatant in their sexuality and were unwilling to repent, I would talk to them any time they wanted to. But if, month after month, they were unwilling to do everything that I asked them to do, then I would say, ... "How would you feel about not taking the sacrament?"[31] ... In high council meeting we talked about kicking them out of the church. We got in a discussion about what's the most grievous sin. It was interesting, they were willing to grade everything—this is the most serious, then this is next, and so on. The Savior says that the least degree of sinners aren't acceptable in God's kingdom. ... It's the *least* degree of sin that is going to keep me out of the kingdom until I'm willing to repent of it. That's the mentality we need to give to people, that we're all sinners.[32]

Shortly after he started serving as bishop, Roberts began to receive calls from LDS Social Services asking his opinion on matters concerning homosexuality. One member of the ward told this researcher:

> [LDS] Social Services was using him [Roberts] as kind of an experiment. They were sort of looking at how things were going to see how it might influence church policy. It was safe for them. A ward in [San Francisco] is a pretty safe place to have a bunch of [gay people] meeting. It was far enough out of Utah that they could scrutinize without being outwardly supportive.

Eventually, LDS Social Services approached Roberts about leading a gay support group comprised of members of the ward. With the permission of the stake president, the group was expanded to include gay men throughout the Bay area. The group met at Roberts' house on Saturdays and discussed issues relating to homosexuality and the church. A newsletter, entitled the *FLaMiNGO News* (an acronym for "Friends, Lovers and Mormons in a Nameless Gay Organization") filled with the proceedings of the meetings and other items was published, and persisted for a while even after the group disbanded.[33]

Despite its novelty, Roberts's experiment was modest in scope and short-lived. Only four months after the formation of the study group, Roberts was released from his calling as bishop of the San Francisco singles ward. (In spite of persistent rumors to the contrary, the release was at Roberts' request and was not disciplinary in nature.)[34] Furthermore, less than 20 men ever participated.

In spite of the meager numbers and short duration, this group had a substantial impact on the thinking of clinicians at LDS Social Services, and Roberts's tolerance of "non-practicing" gay people in his ward foreran a major shift in the way the official church perceives its gay members. Other "experimental" groups, under the watchful eye of church clinicians, were soon to follow. The feelings expressed in these groups began to drive home the message that homosexuality is not amenable to change, and that traditional Mormon teachings about the cause and "treatment" of same sex orientation are untenable.

This new enlightenment did not escape the eyes of liberal Mormons and the LDS intelligentsia, who turned gay rights in the church into their own cause célèbre. A letter to the editor war between those with a traditional Mormon outlook on homosexuality, and those pushing the church for a more progressive stance erupted in the two journals for Mormon scholarship, *Dialogue* and *Sunstone*—both staples on the coffee tables of liberal Mormons. Debates about the roles that gay people can play in the church, and the theological implications of homosexuality all played themselves out in these unofficial, but influential publications. For example, in one issue of *Sunstone*, the following letters appeared:

> When [the author of an article in last month's *Sunstone*] speaks of repenting of homosexual behavior, I find his argument compelling. When he speaks of repenting of homosexuality, I find his argument ridiculous. Homosexuals can no more 'repent' of their homosexuality than I can of my heterosexuality, but we can both refrain from sexual relations and other behaviors that have been proscribed by a faith we subscribe to.[35]

> Only a perverse God would create deep, permanent desire in certain human hearts and then deprive them of and real hope of fulfillment. Let us hope that when Christ comes a second time, we are not surprised to find gays and lesbians entering the Kingdom before we do.[36]

In time, a consensus began to emerge which favored the view that *being* gay is not a sin, but *acting* gay is. (The same view advanced by bishop Stan Roberts.) Eugene England, a former professor of English at BYU and a distinguished Mormon author and poet, summed up this new sentiment, writing:

> The longer I live the more I'm convinced that every human being has at least one cross to bear that he did not 'choose,' and though some, perhaps most, such crosses are not as difficult to bear as homosexuality, some are *more* difficult: Because of accidents, physical appearance, or handicaps many more than 10 percent of humans in our culture are unable to enjoy normal sexual expression and marriage and have to settle for a life devoid of sexual intimacy, even affection. Are they to be excused from any 'charge of sin' if they pursue sexual expression in forbidden or destructive ways, say with prostitutes¿[37]

LDS church leaders and clinicians at social services agreed, and a new handbook on homosexuality to update the 1981 release, was distributed to bishops by the church. In this 1992 booklet, entitled *Understanding and Helping Those Who Have Homosexual Problems*, the First Presidency states that a "single standard of morality" exists within the church: "abstinence outside of lawful marriage and fidelity within marriage." Sexual activity of any other kind—be it homosexual, heterosexual, or autoerotic—is sinful."[38] This single standard of morality does not label gay people as perverts or degenerates, but rather defines homosexual *behavior* as activity that falls outside the range of acceptable sexual expression in the church.

The handbook suggests that the immediate goal for gay Latter-day Saints is to remain chaste. Those who are able to do this may then be able to work on their orientation and inclinations.[39] For gay Mormons, this means that as long as one maintains a celibate lifestyle, one can be a church member in good standing. Celibate men are able to hold priesthood positions, serve missions, and take the sacrament—same-sex attractions notwithstanding—so long as they abstain from sexual activity. This is a departure from earlier statements characterizing thoughts, feelings, and attitudes as sinful. It is also a change from the earlier handbook which demanded a change in sexual orientation. The depth of these changes is illustrated in a side by side comparison between the two handbooks in Table 3.1 below.

TABLE 3.1 CHANGES IN LDS POLICY TOWARD HOMOSEXUAL MEMBERS

HOMOSEXUALITY, 1981	*UNDERSTANDING*, 1992
Homosexuality is erotic physical contact or attractions between members of the same sex, including erotic same sex fantasy. It may include thought or emotional attractions without outward sexual behavior ... (p. 1)	There is a distinction between immoral thought and feelings and participating in either immoral heterosexual and any homosexual behavior. (p. 1)
Encourage the member to be in appropriate situations with members of the opposite sex, even if he has to force himself. If he is single, he might attend activities for singles with increasing frequency ... Encourage him (if single) to begin dating and gradually increase its frequency. (p. 6)	Marriage should not be viewed as a way to resolve homosexual problems. The lives of others should not be damaged by entering a marriage where such concerns exist. Encouraging members to cultivate heterosexual feelings as a way to resolve homosexual problems generally leads to frustration and discouragement. (p. 4)

Many gay Mormons have accepted this compromise, and see the opportunity to live under the "single standard of morality" as a chance to nurture their spirituality within the religious organization they believe to be true. The church has responded in kind, playing down its doctrine of "ministering angel" status for those who die faithful but single. Counselors at Social Services now tell their gay clients that if they live a faithful, celibate life, the Lord will see to it that they will have exaltation. Whether this means that they will be celibate in heaven or whether it means that when Christ returns, those who are gay will become "straight" and hence able to marry is not completely clear. In spite of this ambiguity, one respondent to this study assessed the significance of the church's change of heart thusly:

> Before, I always believed that I could never be saved. Now I think that things will be all right. If I can keep from backsliding I'll be okay. I believe that the Lord will take care of it during the millennium. At least I can go to church and be who I am.

Another, equally accepting of this compromise writes:

> As a gay Latter-day Saint I accept the responsibility to represent both of my communities honorably (as do many others). My temple recommend[40] is valid. While it is no magic qualifier, it means to me that I can answer with an unqualified "yes" to the question, "Are you morally clean?" And only my priesthood leader can ask that question.[41]

The acceptance of gay church members who commit to a celibate lifestyle and the new "single standard of morality" is the most significant change in the history of the Mormon church's policy on homosexuality. The publication of the new handbook drew sufficient attention from the press and public to warrant the appearance of one of the directors of LDS Social Services, Herald Brown, on a Salt Lake City call-in television talk-show to explain the new policy. Brown's response to the very first question was an explanation of the new "single standard" and an assurance that this standard does not discriminate against homosexuals.

> **TALK SHOW HOST:** Some homosexuals would say that you are harming them, that this teaching teaches them that they are second class citizens, that their feelings of love and sex are inferior to other people's feelings of

love and sex, that they are sinful, and that that will end up harming people. Is that so?
HERALD BROWN: I can understand that people do feel that way, but I think homosexuality is best understood within the context of a larger issue of a standard of morality within the church, and that standard is abstinence before marriage and fidelity within marriage. And that's the same standard for every individual within the church.
TALK SHOW HOST: Okay, so you're not picking on homosexuals, you say. You say everyone, no matter what his or her sexual orientation should only have sex in marriage.
HERALD BROWN: That is correct. That is correct. And that is the same standard for all. It is the standard for old, young, single, married, everyone.[42]

At first glance, this notion of a "single standard of morality" seems to be a consistent policy that does not single out the activity of gay people. But, when pressed later in the show by a caller, Brown was forced to admit that the notion of "one standard" is more rationalization than reality.

CALLER: You speak of a standard of morality in the church in which all members, whether heterosexual or homosexual are required to live by. My question is, is the act of holding hands or an affectionate kiss any more grave than that of a heterosexual couple would be?
HERALD BROWN: [Pause] You're talking—you're, uh—one more time, please?
TALK SHOW HOST: [Breaking in] You say the standard is the same. Now, in fact, the church does not frown too much if you kiss your girlfriend. Does it frown if the guy kisses his boyfriend. Is it the same as kissing your girlfriend given that there is a single standard of morality.
HERALD BROWN: Well, I think that would be the beginning of a homosexual act, it may not be the ultimate homosexual act, but it's the beginnings of it. So, yes it would be seen differently from a young man and woman kissing each other.
TALK SHOW HOST: So it isn't quite the same then. It isn't quite one standard of morality. Its okay for a young man and woman to kiss, but it's not okay for a young man and man to kiss.
HERALD BROWN: At that point in time that is the beginning of homosexual behavior.
TALK SHOW HOST: Yeah, but the other is the beginning of heterosexual behavior.
HERALD BROWN: That's correct. But that leads to something that is acceptable in the church. ...
TALK SHOW HOST: I'd say he [the caller] scored a point. It isn't one

> standard. Kissing your girlfriend is okay, kissing your boyfriend is not okay, assuming you're a man.
> **HERALD BROWN:** If you'd like to present it in that fashion, you could grant that.[43]

Thus, in spite of the fact that the LDS church no longer routinely excommunicates homosexuals, many gay church members, liberal Mormons, and outside observers assert that the real change in the church's policy has been one of temperament, not one of substance. Evidence for this stems from the fact that the church is still unwilling to discard its view that homosexuality is freely chosen behavior. Also evident is that while the church does not *force* its homosexual members to change their sexual orientation, it nevertheless believes that change is possible for many, if not most. Herald Brown continues:

> **TALK SHOW HOST:** You don't believe homosexuals were born that way, is that right?
> **HERALD BROWN:** That's correct. Because of the individuals we have seen ... who have been able to eliminate homosexual thoughts, feelings and behavior—as evidence that it can be done we've watched them do it. ... I think it's important, however, to define change, because in the past I think we have, some people have used, for example, the word "cure," which I certainly think is a very inappropriate term. ...[44]
> **TALK SHOW HOST:** It seems to imply that—you say some can—that seems to me some can't. So I guess this booklet envisions a class of people who have homosexual feelings, don't have heterosexual feelings, and while they can refrain from homosexual feelings and thoughts, they probably will never get married and will never live the ordinary LDS life.
> **HERALD BROWN:** I think that's possible.[45]

Informants for this study tell stories consistent with these statements. Most say that their initial counseling experiences with LDS Social Services have involved, as one man puts it, "making a go at playing it straight." Only after consistent failure in these concerted efforts does the gay client begin to hear talk of living and coping with homosexuality. Moreover, there is also significant evidence that LDS Social Services has been courting programs, particularly those sponsored by Evangelical Christian organizations, that prescribe methods for changing sexual orientation. One such program is outlined in a book called *Desires in Conflict*, written by Joe Dallas, the president of an "ex-gay" fundamentalist ministry called Exodus International. Another is entitled, *You Don't Have to be Gay*. The distribution of these books points to the seriousness of the LDS church's commitment to changing the orientation of its gay members, since the Evangelical Protestant theology that pervades their pages is mostly incompatible with Mormon theology.

LDS Social Services also expressed an interest in the Evergreen Foundation, a nonprofit group for "recovered" LDS gay men and lesbians operating in Utah. In spite of specific denials that the church in any way endorsed "reparative therapy" for homosexuals, LDS Social Services officials were among the contributors in the Evergreen Foundation's two-day conference in Salt Lake City.[46] The theme and title of this conference was: "You Don't Have to be Gay: Developing a Healthy Male Identity." One observer noted:

> Although the conference was billed for only those who want to change, it seemed hopeless for this conference to try and transcend the inherent message that all gay persons should change to the better (heterosexual) life. Being gay was viewed as unnatural by God and was therefore presented as sin. ... One clear message from all participants was that it was a tremendous struggle to like yourself as gay within Mormonism. Challengers of the conference felt it was an impossible task to like yourself until you had quit trying to change yourself.[47]

In sum, while the church has responded outwardly to the dilemmas of gay church members with counseling programs and professional clinicians, it still seems loathe to abandon the earlier edicts of apostles and prophets who have said, without equivocation, that homosexuality can (and should) be changed. The gay Mormon who attempts to manage identity conflict and dissonance through Mormon ecclesiastical channels is not likely to miss the fundamentalist undertow that hides barely beneath the new current of tolerance.

Notes

1. Edward Kimball and Andrew E. Kimball, *Spencer W. Kimball* (Salt Lake City: Bookcraft, 1977).
2. Ron Schow, Wayne Schow and Maybeth Raynes, *Peculiar People: Mormons and Same Sex Orientation* (Salt Lake City: Signature Books, 1991), xxv.
3. Kimball, *Miracle of Forgiveness*, 77.

4. Ibid., 79.
5. Ibid., 78.
6. *Homosexuality* (Salt Lake City: Corporation of the President of the Church of Jesus Christ of Latter-day Saints, 1981), 1. An official publication of the First Presidency of the Church of Jesus Christ of Latter-day Saints. A copy is in the author's possession.
7. Ibid., 1.
8. Ibid., 2.
9. *Doctrine and Covenants* 93:29. See also McKonkie, *Mormon Doctrine*, 589–590.
10. *Homosexuality*, 2.
11. Mormons cite First Corinthians 10:13 to support this claim. Moreover, the *Book of Mormon* states: "... the Lord giveth no commandments unto the children of men, save he shall prepare a way for them that they may accomplish the thing which he commandeth them." See 1 Nephi 3:7.
12. *Homosexuality*, 4–9.
13. Ibid., 6.
14. Schow, et al. *Peculiar People*, xxvii. For a discussion of the LDS church and aversion therapy, see chapter 4 in this book.
15. Max Ford McBride, *Effect of Visual Stimuli in Electric Shock Therapy*. Ph.D. Dissertation, Brigham Young University, 1976.
16. Robert Rees, "Bishop Pleads Case for LDS Gays, Lesbians," *Affinity* 13, no. 10 (1991): 1.
17. Carlford Broderick, *One Flesh, One Heart* (Salt Lake City: Deseret Book, 1986), 80.
18. Victor L. Brown, *Fred's Story* (Sacramento, CA: HR Associates, 1985), 13.
19. Jan R. Stout, "Sin and Sexuality: Psychobiology and the Development of Homosexuality." *Dialogue* 20, no. 2 (1987): 29.
20. Grant Cheever, "Self Help" in *Affirmations: A Select Anthology of Writings for Gay and Lesbian Mormons*. (*n.p.*, 1985), 16.
21. *Affirmation Charter*. (*n.p.*, 1990). Membership charter and constitution of the gay Mormon support group Affirmation. A copy is in the author's possession.
22. Ibid.
23. See an untitled news story in *Sunstone* 10, no. 10 (1986): 43–44.
24. This statement is found in an untitled article in the newsletter *Affinity* 13, no. 3 (1991): 3.
25. "Kicking against the pricks" is a Mormon idiom meaning to struggle against righteousness. *Doctrine and Covenants* 121:38 reads: "Behold, ere he is aware, he is left unto himself, to kick against the pricks, to persecute the saints, and to fight against God." The term is originally taken from Acts 9:5 in the New Testament. No double entendre was intended by the informant.
26. A reference to Alma 41:10 in the *Book of Mormon*: "Do not suppose, because it has been spoken concerning restoration, that ye shall be restored from sin to happiness. Behold, I say unto you, wickedness never was happiness."

27. Eric Gottfrid Swedin, *Healing Souls: Psychotherapy in the Latter-day Saint Community* (Urbana, IL: University of Illinois Press, 2003).
28. Stan Roberts, "Pastoring the Farside: Making a Place for Believing Homosexuals" *Sunstone* 14, no. 1 (1990): 13.
29. Ibid.
30. Ibid., 15.
31. The LDS sacrament is a weekly rite, wherein bread and water are served to represent the body and blood of Christ. It is common for a bishop to withhold the blessings of the sacrament for those who are deemed unworthy or who are in the process of repenting for grievous sins.
32. Roberts, "Pastoring the Farside," 15. Emphasis in original.
33. *Affinity* 13, no. 7 (1991): 4.
34. Roberts, "Pastoring the Farside."
35. Arnold V. Loveridge, "Inclining to Caring Acts" *Sunstone* 14, no. 3, (1990): 2.
36. See David Alan Lach, *Homosexuality and Scripture* (Los Angeles: *n.p.*, 1989)
37. Eugene England, "Empathy Not Confusion" *Dialogue: A Journal of Mormon Thought* 20, no. 3 (1987): 6.
38. *Understanding and Helping Those Who Have Homosexual Problems* (Salt Lake City: Church of Jesus Christ of Latter-day Saints, 1992), 1. An official publication of the LDS church. A copy is in the author's possession.
39. Ibid.
40. Entrance to the temple requires a "temple recommend." One can obtain such a document only through strict adherence to the principles of the Church of Jesus Christ of Latter-day Saints, and by being found worthy to enter the temple by successfully passing a searching "interview" with one's bishop.
41. Marty Beaudet, "Homophobic Rameuptoms" *Sunstone* 14, no. 3 (1990): 3.
42. *Take Two*, hosted by Rod Decker. This episode aired on Salt Lake City station KUTV on June 7, 1992.
43. Ibid.
44. One person who used this "very inappropriate term" was the apostle (and later prophet) Spencer W. Kimball, who is quoted on page 31.
45. *Take Two*, June 7, 1992.
46. *Affinity* 13, no. 10 (1991): 1.
47. Chris Allen, "Conference on Changing Gay Orientation Stirs Controversy" *Sunstone* 14, no. 3 (1990): 62.

CHAPTER FOUR
Coming Out within Mormonism

Most gay Latter-day Saints, at the time in their lives when they are first coming to grips with their sexual orientation, do not know that their church has been amending and refining its position on homosexuality for over 40 years. Indeed most, when they first perceive that they are somehow "different," do not know that the church has institutionalized methods for dealing with gay members at all. They know only that their church teaches that homosexual behavior is a grievous sin, and that they are confused, burdened with guilt, and worried that their salvation is in jeopardy.

Homosexuality and Mormon Norms of Sexual Purity

The psychological turmoil that accompanies becoming aware of one's homosexuality is not unique to Mormons, but certain aspects of Mormon culture seem to exacerbate this anxiety and keep gay Latter-day Saints from telling others about their sexual orientation. Wells and Kline point out that young gay people are often anxious about coming out because of fear of rejection and stigma.[1] For this reason, they are usually very selective about who they tell, and typically elicit someone's views on homosexuality before coming out to them. Young Mormons, of course, know exactly where respected church leaders and LDS family members stand on the matter, and are well aware of the stigma attached to gay people in the church.

Moreover, the church's efforts to ensure the sexual purity of its youth compound this fear and trepidation with guilt and shame.

Upholding the church's standards of sexual purity, as defined by Mormon authorities and scripture, is perhaps the most emphasized and frequent message of LDS officials to the youth and single people of the church. Throughout the year, young Mormons hear a number of Sunday school lessons on the dangers of sexual immorality. Girls in the church are warned that worthy men will not want to marry them if they are not virgins, and boys are told that masturbation is an evil practice that can lead to more serious sexual sins.[2]

Outside of Sunday services, young Mormons attend other functions where the importance of sexual purity is regularly stressed. Even ward youth outings such as camping trips or barbecues often close with an inspirational meeting wherein young people are admonished to curtail their sexual behavior and reign in their lustful thoughts. These sentiments are strongly expressed in special meetings for teenage Mormons known as "youth standards nights." Standards nights are normally convened every six months, and they are often intense and emotionally charged affairs. This researcher remembers sitting through many such meetings as a boy while ward leaders, often moved to tears, enumerated the blessings that they have received by living the Lord's "law of chastity."

As standards night comes to a close, young people are given a handbook that outlines the rules for appropriate behavior that youth in the church are expected to follow. It covers everything from the LDS position on rock music to the kinds of activities that are appropriate on Sunday. Regarding homosexuality, this handbook is unequivocal: "Homosexual and lesbian activities are sinful and an abomination to the Lord."[3]

Young Mormons are reminded of these rules from other media as well. Along with meetings and gatherings, the church also fosters a cottage industry of inspirational books for youth. These books are widely available from LDS booksellers, and many deal with the subject of sexual immorality. One book, written for teenage Mormons and a widely read best seller, states:

> The unholy transgression of homosexuality is either rapidly growing, or tolerance is giving it wider publicity. If one has such desires and tendencies, he overcomes them the same as if he had the urge toward petting or fornication or adultery. The Lord condemns and forbids this practice with

> a vigor equal to his condemnation of adultery and other such sexual acts. And the church will excommunicate as readily any unrepentant addict.[4]

The content of much of the church's communication with its teenage members centers on the appropriate ways for them to manage their sexual urges. And, in this context, young Mormons learn very early on how the church feels about homosexuality. Not surprisingly, for many of the informants in this study, the process of recognizing their homosexuality was a very difficult one, characterized by confusion and isolation. As one informant points out:

> There was literally no one to talk to about it. There was nothing I could say. I had never been with a man, but I knew that when I had wet dreams and stuff, all my dreams were about guys. I was going to church and living the commandments, so I couldn't figure out how this could be. I once asked my seminary teacher[5] if I was accountable for the things in my dreams. He figured that they were just ordinary sex dreams I guess, because he told me no. [He said that] the Lord was preparing my body for procreation after I got married. I couldn't go any further and tell him about the details of my dreams. I didn't know if I was sinning or not, but it sure felt like I was.

Another gay Mormon writes:

> Growing up gay and Mormon is many times a very lonely experience. Tonight, in cities and towns across the country, there are gay and lesbian Mormons who are crying out to themselves and to God, asking, "Why am I like this?" They think they are unique—the only ones who have these feelings.[6]

For most gay boys in the church, the isolation associated with being gay is almost always accompanied by guilt and shame over their thoughts and feelings. Most of the men in this study revealed that the anguish they felt over their sexual awakening began long before any overt homosexual experience. They had been effectively taught by the church that unclean thoughts were sins in and of themselves—and these teachings, in most cases, had been successfully internalized. Many feared for their salvation not because they had had illicit homosexual relations, but because they thought or fantasized about such relations. Some informants went to great lengths to attempt to suppress their emerging homosexuality:

> I had an elaborate scheme developed to keep me from thinking about [sex with men]. I remembered a talk by an apostle that said that our minds are a stage and our thoughts are actors on the stage and that evil players are always trying to take the stage and entertain us. So when they are about to take the stage, you should have the words to a hymn or a favorite scripture memorized to chase them away.[7] I had the words to Ether 12:27[8] memorized. It would chase away the evil characters all right, but I had no idea how persistent they were. My weakness never became a strength, I could never stop thinking about men.

Others in the study reported that in order to avoid homosexual thoughts they immersed themselves in their homework or job.[9] Still others steadily increased their participation in church activities and individual study within the church. One man recalled that he began a regimen of prayer and fasting, denying himself food every Sunday "for a whole month of Sundays." Another recounts that

> I began an agonizing and relentless effort to change. I obeyed all the counsel of the church explicitly and faithfully. No one could have been more determined or confident. It was an absolute desire. Prayer, fasting and faithful allegiance to the church were to the spirit and the letter. I developed stomach ulcers as a result and came close to bleeding to death several times before doctors could get the hemorrhaging stopped.[10]

Wayne Schow, a Mormon whose son died of AIDS in 1986, writes:

> [My son] told us he had prayed fervently over a long period that God would help him to reorient his sexual feelings, and in return he promised God extraordinary devotion. His personal journals from this period reveal a religious youth caught up in seminary instruction, who concluded from all the implicit messages of home, church and society, that he was flawed and sinful—cursed, as it seemed to him—in spite of his wish to be otherwise.[11]

Most informants said that homosexual thoughts and the emergence of same-sex attractions filled them with guilt, but when these thoughts and fantasies were combined with masturbation, the guilt and shame became debilitating. Masturbation is a concern to the LDS church, and talks by church authorities cautioning young men against it are common. This researcher, like any other church-going Mormon boy, remembers chapels and classrooms filled with nervous and fidgety youths being told that they will be unworthy to serve a mission or enter the temple if they do not repent and forsake masturbation. Young people are also told that masturbation can lead to other forms of sexual perversion. Spencer W. Kimball, twelfth prophet of the Mormon church, wrote: "Sometimes masturbation is the introduction to the more serious sin of exhibitionism and the gross sin of homosexuality."[12]

In fact, several informants reported that they believed their inability to control masturbation was the cause of their homosexuality. While some were more or less successful in their attempts to eliminate or reduce the frequency of masturbation, most admitted that they would inevitably "slip up," no matter how fervent and dedicated their commitment to quit. One man recounted that "I was terrified, because I had promised God that he could send me to hell if I ever did it again."

Self-inflicted mental or physical punishments for masturbating were common among informants. Most prevalent among these punishments were periods of fasting. Some, however, assigned themselves a more unique penance. Jenkins reports that a young man told him that, "as a teenager he had tried drinking hot mustard to destroy his homosexual urges." He further notes that "many kinds of self-punishment have been attempted, from drinking raw eggs to burning oneself."[13] Carl, a student at a Utah university, also admitted that he punished himself for masturbating:

> **INFORMANT:** I would try and resist, but after a while it would be impossible. After a week or so I would always give in.
> **RESEARCHER:** Would you think about men while you masturbated?
> **INFORMANT:** Always. And when I was done I would be filled with self-loathing. My mind would change 180 degrees just like that [snaps fingers].
> **RESEARCHER:** How long did this go on?
> **INFORMANT:** A year. I would always end up giving in when I went to the bathroom because I shared a bedroom with my little brother. There were so many kids in my house that the only time you could be alone was in the bathroom. I would ... [pause] I would feel so bad that I would punish myself. I would wash my hands in the foul water after I had used the toilet. You know, to show God that I felt dirtier than shit. That happened over and over again. I usually felt okay after. For the first little while I felt

> that my punishment was enough, but when I couldn't stop altogether I began to think that maybe I should kill myself.

Suicidal thoughts were quite common among informants, and several admitted to an attempt. Moreover, the prevalence of suicidal thinking among these men seemed to be linked to Mormonism's unique doctrine of repentance. The church teaches that part of the process of repentance is never committing the sinful act again. In order to be forgiven, immoral deeds must be forsaken and abandoned for good. The *Doctrine and Covenants*, a book of Mormon scripture, states: "By this shall ye know if a man repenteth of his sins—behold, he will confess them and forsake them."[14] Spencer W. Kimball further notes that "the discontinuance must be a permanent one. True repentance does not permit repetition."[15] Indeed, several informants mentioned that it was not individual acts of masturbation or particular instances of homosexual fantasizing that prompted their suicidal feelings, but rather the combined weight of many such instances, incompletely repented, bearing down upon them. The notion that this "cumulative burden of sin," as one gay Mormon put it, was of such gravity that its seriousness was equated with the taking of one's own life was a recurrent theme among them.

> Part of repentance is never doing it again. So while I felt okay for a time, when I could see that my efforts were doing no good, then I felt as though all my past sins were on me together. I felt like I was filling the hole I had dug for myself with a spoon, while Satan was digging me deeper with a backhoe! I thought a lot about killing myself.

> I never stopped struggling, but I was so emotionally lacerated ... that I deeply wanted to die. I thought about it so often. I had felt that repressing my homosexual feelings was becoming increasingly impossible and that suicide would be less of a sin than acting out these feelings.[16]

> I thought each time I repented that I would never do it [masturbate while fantasizing about men] again. I was so sure. I was crushed and broken each time I gave in. It is kind of like having bills that exceed your income. You get deeper and deeper in. When the time comes to pay the piper, you either declare bankruptcy, or kill yourself. Neither option is a winner.

> I felt so guilty that I sometimes contemplated suicide, because I couldn't stop—no matter how hard I tried. Not that I would ever do it with a

> man, I knew I could resist that temptation, but that I could not stop myself from thinking about men or having images of men appear before me when I was by myself. ... I [would try to] avoid masturbation as long as I could, but after about three or four months or so I would always break down. Sometimes it wasn't that way at all, though. Sometimes I didn't have any choice at all. Sometimes it was like idle moments when [thoughts about] sex creep into your head like any other person, or when I was asleep. I would dream about men. So I figured I would be in the lower kingdom anyway, whether I killed myself or continued with these thoughts. That's why I contemplated suicide. I just said to myself, 'Either I go the bishop and confess, or I kill myself and settle for the lower heaven.'

The need to confess one's sins to the bishop is usually what brings a gay youth's homosexuality to the attention of the church. Informants who had confessed their "sin" to the bishop said that they sought out church leaders for help because of the weighty burden of guilt and shame they were bearing. Most recall an urgent desire to change their sexual orientation, and a belief that the church and its inspired ecclesiastical leaders was their last, best hope.

Bishops usually become aware of a ward member's homosexuality in one of two ways. First, it may be discovered during the course of a regular priesthood interview. Bishops conduct searching evaluative interviews with the with the young men of the church at six-month intervals, beginning when these boys are first ordained to the priesthood[17] at age 12. Interviews are designed to ensure the moral integrity of the youth of the church, and questions about sexual purity—particularly masturbation—are almost always a part of the discussion. When asked, many boys admit to masturbation, and probing by the bishop can often lead the interviewee to confess to homosexual inclinations as well.

Although lying to the bishop is commonplace, such lies are seen as a serious sin, and sooner or later the guilt from lying, coupled with the guilt and shame from masturbation and homosexual feelings, will compel the young man to confess. Moreover, Mormon youth folklore is replete with stories of the Holy Ghost whispering to inspired bishops and revealing those who lie during priesthood interviews. Many young Mormons harbor a fear that the bishop will know if they are lying. The structure of the ward, and the frequency and intensity of the interaction among ward youth leaders and parents often contributes to this belief, since these networks ensure that bishops are often privy to a great deal of information that young people may not know they possess.

More often, however, informants stated that they sought out the bishop voluntarily to confess their sins, hoping that this step would at last allow them to forsake these transgressions once and for all. This was especially the case among those who had had a homosexual encounter of some sort, since the church teaches that certain serious sins cannot be forgiven until they are openly confessed to ecclesiastical leaders.

Those who approached their bishops intending to confess did so with great trepidation. Many reported that they thought they would be excommunicated when they revealed the truth about their homosexuality—whether or not they had engaged in homosexual acts. The process of excommunication is administered through a church court, and being excommunicated can make one a pariah in Mormon circles, even though most who suffer this fate can rejoin the church after a probationary period. In spite of this, many informants went to their bishops shortly after they realized they were gay, and that they could not fix the problem on their own.

Nevertheless, some informants stated that during their early and mid teen years—a time when bishop's interviews occur with great frequency—they were unaware of their homosexuality. Said one, "I could tell that there was something different about me, but I just couldn't put a finger on what that difference was. I was just confused about my sexuality, but I didn't know I was gay." Others echoed these sentiments, saying that they neither felt the need to lie to their bishop nor seek him out to repent because although they sensed, as one put it, that "something was awry," they did not fully understand what they were going through.

This confusion, reported by several men in the study, is consistent with studies showing that the discovery of homosexuality and the development of a homosexual identity is a process, and does not happen overnight. Troiden writes that the "ideal type" of this identity assumption process involves four distinct steps: (1) sensitization, or the beginning of sexual awareness that accompanies puberty; (2) identity confusion, or the realization that one is "different;" (3) identity assumption, wherein that difference is understood as homosexuality; and (4) commitment, the stage where a homosexual identity becomes permanently incorporated into the individual's personality.[18] Going through this process can take some time, and scholars point out that the "average male homosexual does not identify himself as 'gay' until the ages of nineteen to twenty-one."[19] Trevor, a graduate student in the behavioral sciences at BYU, discussed why it took him until age twenty to recognize his homosexuality:

> When young people of heterosexual preference start to feel their sexual awakenings they have pre-made roles to step into. Heterosexual gender roles. You know, dating and stuff. In the [Mormon] church those roles are especially well defined. Not the gay person, especially not the gay Mormon. Some of them do what I did: they step falteringly into the straight roles, always wondering why they don't quite fit. That's the way I was. It didn't make sense to me until my mission. Then it slapped me in the face. I think if gay Mormons don't know they are gay there is no mistaking it if they serve a mission.

Homosexuality and Missionary Service

If the scholars' estimates are accurate, and Trevor's experience typical among gay Latter-day Saints, the ramifications are profound, since from exactly age nineteen to age twenty-one, young men in the church are commanded to serve a Mormon mission—a two-year period of church service wherein those called as missionaries seek to win converts to the faith.[20] Young Mormon boys begin preparing to serve their mission when they are small by memorizing scriptures and learning songs that glorify missionary life. The mission call often takes a young man thousands of miles from home, and sometimes involves learning a foreign language.

The mission experience is highly regimented. Explicit rules govern virtually every aspect of missionary life, such as when to get up in the morning, what color of shirt to wear, when and how often one can use the telephone, when and under what circumstances a missionary can drive an automobile, and many others.[21] For the purposes of this study, the most interesting set of mission rules are those regulating missionary companionships.

Missionaries live together in designated proselytizing areas with their assigned companions. Throughout the course of their missions, missionaries, or "elders," as they are called, will typically have several areas of service and seven or eight different companions. It is against mission rules to leave the presence of one's companion. Indeed, missionaries may not leave their companion's sight, except to shower or use the bathroom. In cases where a companionship resides in a two bedroom apartment, mission rules require that they share a single room.

Companionships often evolve into stalwart friendships, and this close, intimate contact with other young men was cited as a major frustration by informants who had served a mission. This same close association also forced many who were not fully aware of their homosexuality into the realization that they were, in fact, gay.

> My trainer[22] was the most magnificent person I had ever met. He had an irresistible personality. At first I was filled with hope and peace because he inspired me to work hard and teach the gospel with the Spirit. But my hopes were destroyed when I started to fall in love with him. We were like a normal companionship. You know, when we would come home and get ready for bed he would undress in front of me just like any other normal companion—just roommates, no big deal. I thought to myself that I must not have the Spirit or I wouldn't have these thoughts. It was torture and I became very depressed and homesick. I finally figured out what was wrong with me all this time.

> I had always wondered about whether or not I was gay, but after about two months into my mission there was no doubt. I had never been with men in such close quarters, and the feelings that I felt were just like the feelings that [ward youth leaders] said I should be feeling for girls. I decided then and there that I would use my mission to live the commandments and turn straight ... [But] I had about the same type of feelings with each new companion. I would get aroused when I heard them in the shower because I knew they were naked. Then I would start to feel guilty.

Ironically, the practice of keeping companions within sight of one another at all times is intended to prevent them from getting in trouble with girls.[23]

For those who were already aware of their sexual preference when they received their mission call, being gay did not temper their desire to serve. Moreover, those who had previously confessed to their bishops about homosexual inclinations were not discouraged from going, provided they had not had a serious homosexual encounter. One man recalls:

> My mission call to Japan came in the fall of 1970. During the week I spent in the old mission home[24] in Salt Lake City, we heard among the many inspiring messages given to us by various general authorities of the church some terrifying ones about the evils of unrepentant sexual sin. The word which I could barely say to myself was repeated several times. Homosexuality, we were warned, was consummate evil, and any unrepentant person was doomed to a mission filled with spiritual darkness and failure. I was certain they were right, and with my heart pounding, I requested to speak to the Mission Home president. Upon hearing my confession he assured me that I was involved in the darkest of sins. But after questioning me about specific instances and people I had been involved with, he determined that since I had only homosexual feelings but no experience, I was clean and worthy to go on my mission. I left ... determined to be the best missionary that I could be.[25]

Informants report that the opportunity to serve a mission was seen as an excellent chance to put off the carnal world and cleanse themselves of their homosexual thoughts and feelings. Many believed that serving in such a controlled, spiritual environment would finally cure them of their homosexuality. Jenkins writes:

> I filled a successful mission but was disheartened to return, realizing that my prayers for change remained unanswered. I had felt confident that through complete devotion to the Lord on a mission I would be blessed in return with the fulfillment of the greatest desire of my heart.[26]

Like Jenkins, most informants report that their mission experience only intensified and solidified their homosexual inclinations—in spite of the fact that accounts of actual homosexual encounters between missionaries appear to be rare.[27]

Nevertheless, near encounters or incidents of masturbation accompanied by homosexual fantasizing were often enough to send a missionary to his mission president[28] to confess. Approaching the mission president to confess is reportedly at least as terrifying as confessing to the ward bishop, because missionaries who are guilty of serious sins are subject to severe and extraordinarily stigmatizing punishments. Those who confess to an attraction for a companion are almost always transferred to a new companion. Sometimes this transfer occurs on the regular mission transfer day, which comes up once a month. But if the mission president feels that the need for a transfer is urgent, the move may take place between transfer dates—a signal to the other elders that something is very wrong.[29] Being transferred mid-month carries a heavy stigma among missionaries.

Those who engage in homosexual activity while serving their missions may also be sent home, often to a church court if the encounter is a serious one. Being sent home from a mission is particularly disgraceful, especially in Utah communities and other areas where there is a high concentration of Mormons.

Aside from repenting of sins through voluntary confessions, missionaries are urged to tell the mission president if their companion is engaged in any wrongdoing. Gay elders who do not confess but are caught by their companion doing something wrong, or who admit their homosexual feelings in confidence to a companion are usually summoned for an interview by the mission president. One former missionary recalls:

> **INFORMANT:** The Z.L.'s[30] were in town and needed a place to stay so they stayed with us. We only had two beds so the companionships doubled up in the beds. The lights were off and we were talking and laughing in bed. It was like a sleep over. I started feeling strange [pause] you know. My companion sort of moved in the bed and brushed up against me. You know, he sort of brushed up against me.
> **RESEARCHER:** What do you mean?
> **INFORMANT:** He brushed up against my body, and he could tell, I mean, do you know what I mean?
> **RESEARCHER:** He turned in the bed or something and felt your lower body?
> **INFORMANT:** Yeah.
> **RESEARCHER:** And you had an erection?
> **INFORMANT:** Yeah.
> **RESEARCHER:** Then what happened?
> **INFORMANT:** He stopped talking and everything. I could tell he was freaked out and the next day [the mission president] called up and told me we were going to have a transfer. So everyone in the mission knew something was up. Then I had an interview and [the mission president] asked me if I liked guys. I couldn't lie. I wasn't mad at my companion though. I was glad because I thought that now I could make a change. I had felt so gross before, and then I thought that I could change. Even though everybody thought bad of me I thought that I was better off. It lifted a weight off my shoulders.

Encountering Homosexual Members: Initial Church Reactions

Studies show that outside Mormonism, friends and family are typically the first to learn of someone's homosexuality, but in the LDS church, gay people are more likely to "come out" to their ward bishop or mission president. Voluntary confession for the purpose of repentance is the most common way that church leaders discover that one of their charges is a homosexual. And more often than not, these leaders are also the first ones in whom the gay Mormon confides. Hence, for gay church members, the experience of coming out is very different than for most non-Mormon homosexuals. In the LDS community, coming out does not signify the acceptance of a new identity or a reconciliation with one's homosexuality, but rather an attempt to repent of sin or a plea for help in changing one's sexual orientation.

This pattern certainly holds true for most of the informants in this study, and especially so for those reporting deep religious convictions. One man, describing himself as "completely committed to gospel ideals," states: "as I had done during my entire life, I turned first to the church."[31] Moreover, those from observant homes with highly religious parents were more likely to say that they sought help from church leaders rather than family members, not only because of Mormon ideas about the process of repentance, but also to spare their parents the stigma and shame of having a homosexual son. One man said:

> My parents wouldn't have been able to handle it. They were, and are, very devout. So even though I didn't like my bishop all that much I had no choice. I had to talk to somebody, but it couldn't be my parents. I even worried about the bishop because I feared that he would betray my confidence and tell my folks. It would have been the end of the world for my mother to find out that her son was gay. What am I talking about? She did find out—years later—and it *was* the end of the world. I guess I knew what I was doing, huh?

Whenever a gay Mormon approaches the bishop to confess homosexual thoughts and feelings, or an actual homosexual encounter, the church has a fairly uniform and predictable response. That response, however, has evolved as the church has softened its position on homosexuality over the years.

Among older informants in the study, the most common initial reaction of their bishops was confusion or embarrassment. Most bishops simply did not understand what they were being told.

> That was about 1968. No one had even heard of the word 'gay' as we use it now back then. My bishop just sort of looked at me. If I would have actually [had a homosexual encounter] it might have been different, but I was just confessing about my thoughts. I don't think that he really understood what I was trying to tell him. I had tears streaming down my face and I was pleading with him and he just sort of looked at me. After a while, he said that he would have to call the stake president and that he would get back with me. He didn't know what to do.

According to this research, few bishops in the late 1960s and early 70s—which is as far back as information from these interviews can reliably go—were prepared to deal with the emotional and psychological needs of the gay parishioners who approached them with their problems, and fewer still few were familiar with scientific explanations for the nature and causes of homosexuality. A professor at a Utah university who served as a bishop from 1966 to 1972 explains:

> Although I had heard of homosexuality, it was mostly in the context of how Gibbon[32] viewed it! I fully believed that it was an act of depravity, sort of the last rung on the ladder of personal, moral decay. My response to the young man in my office was that we would have to convene a church court, even though the offense was just kissing and homosexual petting. ... Then I assured him that he would not be excommunicated for such an offense, and that there was hope for forgiveness. Then I just kind of told him "Go thy way and sin no more."[33] He seemed extremely sincere about asking for forgiveness and was absolutely wracked with guilt. That is why a few weeks later I was stunned to learn that had been involved in another homosexual incident. I just didn't understand what being gay was all about.

Others told tales similar to this anecdote, and evidence suggests that in the years before the church published its first handbook dealing with homosexuality, the most common consequence for those who confessed any sort of homosexual activity was some form of disciplinary action, usually in the form of a church court.

Sociologists of religion note that in order to maintain the orthodoxy of believers and uphold consensus in matters of faith and doctrine, religious organizations may resort to coercive means of controlling their members. In the Mormon church, coercive control is exercised through the use of sanctions which limit participation in church activities and sacraments. There are three levels of disciplinary sanction. The most mild of these is called "probation." Probation is usually fairly informal and involves an agreement between the bishop and the censured party to refrain from taking the weekly bread and water communion, and to stop attending the temple until the probation has been lifted. Probation does not typically involve a formal church court, but rather a series of meetings between the bishop and the church member.

More serious is "disfellowshipment," which is an institutional sanction administered by a church court. Disfellowshipped members are allowed to attend church meetings, but cannot have ward callings and may not participate in priesthood ordinances or partake of the sacrament. The ultimate punishment meted out by church courts is excommunication.

One former bishop reported that, in his experience as a bishop from 1963 to 1970 in a small Utah town,

> I saw a number of young men who had [homosexual problems]. Those who had had only one experience or just a very few might usually just get a probation period, provided that they hadn't gone very far. Also, I felt it was the Lord's will to go easier on Aaronic priesthood holders than on Melchizedek priesthood[34] brethren. But if a young man had a lot of involvement or had had [oral or anal sex, then the person] would almost certainly be at least disfellowshipped. Melchizedek priesthood holders who [had engaged in such activities] were excommunicated, but those punishments weren't up to me, they were meted out by church courts.

The response of bishops in the 1960s and 1970s to those who had not had homosexual experiences, but were nevertheless vexed by their sexual thoughts is somewhat less uniform, but almost always involved directing the person toward more "masculine" behaviors. Some informants stated that when they confessed their homosexual feelings and inclinations, their bishops dismissed their problems as a phase, telling them not to worry, and declaring that "nature [will] take over in relatively short order." One man reports that his bishop merely "assured me that what I needed to do was to continue to date girls, participate fully in church activity, and follow the commandments."[35]

But when tormented youths who received such advice returned to ward leaders for subsequent visits, bishops began to make suggestions and concoct strategies for reorienting homosexual thoughts.

Most informants who approached their bishops during this time period note that ward leaders often suggested that they do more "manly" things, apparently in the belief that homosexuality was caused by effeminate attitudes. One informant said: "He [my bishop] told me I should begin exercising more, that I should hike or play baseball." Particularly common were exhortations to begin practicing with the ward basketball team.[36] One writer, recalling a counseling session with a general authority, writes:

> As a final thought he suggested that I might aim for more masculine activities in life, such as playing basketball. The advice was given in good faith and was appreciated. But I wondered if he saw the dilemma. Had I confessed to heterosexual problems, would he have prescribed more physical contact with girls, culminating in the showers?[37]

One puzzling datum, reported frequently by older informants, was that bishops and church leaders advised them that homosexual desires and the urge to masturbate were heightened by wearing briefs. Fred reports that in the mid 1970s, his bishop "asked me if I wore briefs or boxers. I told him briefs and he said that I should switch." And Roger states that his bishop "told me that my manhood needed to breathe, that I was probably having difficulty because I was wearing underwear that was too small for me."

The origin of this strange bit of counsel is unknown, but logic dictates that it must come from some official or semi-official source, since it came up frequency among older informants.[38] Jenkins's narrative provides further evidence of this. He reports that in the early seventies, a general authority of the church "counseled me to ... think manly thoughts, be faithful to the church, and not to wear tight pants."[39]

Weeks or months later, when gay ward members returned to their bishops complaining that looser shorts and participation in organized sports had not curbed their homosexual desires, bishops typically began counseling the young men to begin heterosexual dating. If the counselee was already seeing a young woman, he was encouraged to increase the seriousness of the relationship, and the level of physical affection within it. As Mitchell remembers:

> Finally he [the bishop] told me that all I needed to do was to get with some girls and start dating. He said that at first it might be hard, but that in the end my instincts would fix the problem. He said that [homosexual attractions were] unnatural and that seeing girls would fix it.

Those who were able to successfully manage a heterosexual relationship and who had completed a mission were typically advised to marry as soon as possible. Older informants report that they received considerable pressure from church leaders to marry, and most say that they were instructed not to tell their potential spouse that they were gay. This advice was given by a general authority to a gay man who writes: "He [the authority] asked me to picture myself capable of [heterosexual love making.] ... He felt I should marry but counseled me definitely not to tell my wife I was a homosexual as it would strain the relationship too severely."[40] Many did marry, and the results, as chapter five demonstrates, were disastrous.

The final and most dramatic method used by the church to try and change the sexual orientation of gay members was "negative behavioral" or "aversion" therapy. Aversion therapy employs the principles of behavioral psychology to attempt to change a homosexual person's sexual preference through negative reinforcement. Church-owned Brigham Young University conducted a great deal of research throughout the 1970s in order to determine the relative merits of aversion therapy in "treating" gay people.[41]

Homosexual men became participants in these reconditioning studies in one of two ways. A few were referred by bishops, stake presidents, and mission presidents who were familiar with this research, but most were BYU students who approached the university's counseling center for help with emotional problems. Some said that they approached counselors specifically to discuss homosexuality, while others said that they initially sought help for other problems, and that their sexual orientation came out during the course of therapy.

After some searching, the researcher managed to speak with several people who participated in aversion therapy experiments. Each recalled that they began their participation in these projects by going through a period of counseling, often including hypnosis and group therapy. Then, when the experiments in aversion therapy began, they were shown homoerotic photographs while painful electric shocks were administered. One man who endured this therapy recounts:

> Random and painful electric shocks would be sent through my arm. Later the procedure was modified. When shock was being introduced during the viewing of a male slide, I could stop the shock by pressing a plunger, which would cause the slide of a clothed woman to appear on the screen. Even now other details of the therapy are too embarrassing for me to write about.[42]

Participants in the experiments were often told in counseling sessions that they were making excellent progress, although one man notes that "the criteria used by my counselor to determine whether or not I was cured of homosexuality were not clear to me."[43] In spite of this, those who participated left their therapy feeling that nothing had changed, in spite of assurances from those administering the experiments that they had been "cured."

Aversion therapy experiments began to taper off at BYU, both because they were a failure, and because the APA was becoming increasingly critical of such therapeutic techniques. By 1983, only remnants of the program remained. Faced with the realization that the program did not work, and that there seemed to be no way to change homosexuality into heterosexuality (and newly beset by outspoken gay Mormons who demanded better treatment) the church began to lighten up on gay members who approached their ecclesiastical leaders for repentance and help.

Younger informants report a very different experience in the bishop's office than their older counterparts, especially those who approached their bishops beginning in the 1990s. While initial visits still involved exhortations to "play it straight," show up for ward basketball practice, and have regular, sincere personal prayer, those who return to the bishop's office insisting that they are gay are promptly referred to LDS Social Services or an LDS counselor. It then becomes the counselor's job to assist the young man in managing his homosexuality and maintaining his mental health, while the bishop's sole concern is the individual's personal worthiness.

Most informants in this era were surprised and impressed at how sincere and solicitous bishops were as they listened to their problems. Rather than the expected condemnation and the threat of excommunication, most reported that the bishop expressed his concern, and provided assurance that the church would not turn its back on them, provided that they put forth a sincere effort to live the commandments.

Today, an individual who approaches his bishop for help dealing with homosexuality is rarely brought before a church court, unless his homosexual experiences are very extensive, he has AIDS, he is a transsexual or undergoing a sex change operation, or he holds a position of high responsibility in the church. Even then, the usual outcome of a church court is disfellowshipment rather than excommunication, provided the person is penitent and commits to live by the moral standards of the church.

Because of this more relaxed atmosphere, many gay people who are in good standing with the church are more or less out of the closet to a select few in their wards, although many continue to keep their sexual orientation hidden from their families. Some even have church callings, though none are allowed to work with the youth or hold high positions with considerable responsibility, like serving in the bishopric. All, of course, must be committed to and working toward changing their sexual orientation, or, short of that, living a celibate lifestyle. The words of one gay Mormon typify the recent experience of gay people who are willing to change or live celibate within the church:

> I recently came out to my bishop, stake president, elder's quorum president and single adult leaders, plus several LDS friends, and none of them has ever said anything terrible to me. I was released as a single adult representative because of my orientation, yet the singles chairperson encouraged me to keep coming to the council meetings because they need ideas.[44]

In spite of this new climate of compromise, the pressure on gay Mormons is still intense. In the interests of safeguarding the personal worthiness of ward priesthood holders, bishops will assist a gay church member in his struggle to remain celibate by inviting him to frequent and searching interviews. These interviews never fail to assess the prevalence and intensity of homosexual thoughts, and the frequency of masturbation. Mark, a freshman at a private college in Salt Lake, states:

> **INFORMANT:** I see him [the bishop] every other week for about a half hour. We talk about my scripture reading and fasting. He asks me everything. It keeps me safe from doing anything wrong, but I am so worried about my next interview that I spend all my time making sure that I'm not thinking or acting gay. It takes a lot of effort.
> **RESEARCHER:** Do you ever have a problem with masturbation?
> **INFORMANT:** Now you're starting to sound like him.
> **RESEARCHER:** No, [laughs] it's just a concern that some others have had.
> **INFORMANT:** It's hard on me. That's all I can say. I don't know how much longer I can live like this.
> **RESEARCHER:** What will you do? Do you think you can [change your sexual orientation?].
> **INFORMANT:** No, they want me to keep this up for the rest of my life.
> **RESEARCHER:** Is that realistic?
> **INFORMANT:** I don't know what to do. I know that gospel is true, but I also know that I can't change what I am. I mean, the people at LDS Social Services know that too. What they want me to do is to live like this forever.
> **RESEARCHER:** Celibate?
> **INFORMANT:** Yeah.
> **RESEARCHER:** Well, can you?
> **INFORMANT:** Could you?

Submitting to a battery of interviews is standard fare for those who want to keep their church membership intact, and several informants reported that "life under a microscope" is stressful. Richard, for instance, decided that it would be easier to claim to be "cured" than to continue his weekly interviews with his bishop. But, in order to make the claim believable, he had to begin dating a woman in the ward.

Reasons for a Policy Shift

Paradoxically, while the church began to lighten up on the treatment of gay members in bishop's offices beginning in the 1990s, church rhetoric and the condemnation of homosexuality from the pulpit and in church printed matter did not relax at all. Throughout the 1990s, official publications and textbooks used in LDS Institute[45] classes continued to claim that sexual sins like homosexual behavior are "precariously close" to murder in their seriousness.[46] This begs the question of why a church that had so few qualms about excommunicating homosexual members in the 1970s decided to keep these same people as members in good standing (under certain conditions) beginning in the 1990s—especially when the church's view of homosexuality did not soften a bit. Certainly the pressure placed on the church by a society with rapidly liberalizing views on sexual matters played a part, but interviews with bishops and gay Mormons revealed that, while national trends may have been an accommodating backdrop for these changes, they are not the immediate cause of this policy shift.

Bishops report that a major reason why gay members are less likely to face church courts today is because most of those who were being excommunicated were not returning to the church. As noted above, after a minimum one year waiting period, those who have been stripped of church membership are eligible, if they have successfully repented, to be rebaptized into the church. Rebaptism carries with it all of the blessings of one's original baptism, including the remission of all sin previous to the ordinance. Thus, for the church, excommunication is seen as the easiest, best way to secure forgiveness of very serious transgressions. This is why Mormon idiom refers to church courts as "courts of love," because they facilitate complete repentance. One bishop remarked:

> The problem is, most people can't face the other members of the church and aren't strong enough to admit to their peers that they have sinned, even though the scriptures teach that all have sinned. None of them were coming back to the church. The church's first obligation is to save mankind, and if a church policy is not helping people be saved, then the Lord will allow it to be changed. You can't be saved outside the gospel. Since I've been a bishop, we have only had one excommunication that wasn't asked for by the person or where the person didn't desire repentance, and that was for child sex abuse. So it isn't just for gay people. People usually don't get excommunicated for adultery or fornication anymore either, unless they ask or are not remorseful. I think that they should ask sometimes, because a contemplative year without the blessings of the gospel can do more toward keeping a member faithful to the end than the years and years it might take to repent without a court of love. But, so be it. Once again the people of the church choose to live a lower law and by doing so they deny themselves blessings.

Another reason why gay Mormons are rarely excommunicated these days stems from LDS beliefs about the sanctity of the family. Shepherd and Shepherd write that preserving the nuclear family in the wake of perceived threats has become "the major sociological frame of reference for [LDS general] conference speakers. The Mormon church is portrayed as serving the basic needs of the family, and the family in turn is defined as the basis of the church."[47] Shipps notes that because of Mormonism's unique doctrine of eternal marriage and the practice of "sealing" children to their parents in temple ceremonies, the "family is [Mormonism's] 'unit of exaltation' rather than the individual."[48] Indeed, one of Mormonism's most familiar and ubiquitous aphorisms is: "families are forever." This slogan appears frequently in the sermons of church leaders, on wall hangings in Mormon homes, and, in places where there is a high concentration of Mormons, on bumper stickers and license plate frames.

The problem is, in order for an entire family to be "forever," all of its members must be individually exalted as well. Homosexuality threatens personal exaltation and, by implication, family exaltation. When pressed by the researcher, bishops admitted to a great deal of deliberation when deciding how to handle homosexual members, in spite of fairly rigid official guidelines. "I have to protect the priesthood and make sure that its members are worthy," said one, "but I must also preserve the family." Thus, excommunicating homosexual members has ramifications on the worthy members of the gay person's family. This, more than anything else, has lead to the church's decision not to excommunicate homosexuals and, more importantly, to accept those living a celibate lifestyle rather than demanding a change in sexual orientation.

Studies show that while joining a radical cult movement, suicide, and committing a felony are all negatively correlated with church membership in the United States, homosexuality is not.[49] What this means is that orthodox, devout Mormon families are just as likely to have to deal with a gay family member as their less religious counterparts. The implications of this are obvious when one examines the speeches and teachings of Mormon leaders on causes of deviance in the family.

Mormonism, Homosexuality, and Families

The preservation of the nuclear family is modern Mormonism's most celebrated message. Cowan points out that the precipitous rise in divorce rates immediately following World War II prompted church leaders to begin emphasizing the primacy of the family as the bedrock unit of society and the church. Joseph Fielding Smith, tenth president of the LDS church, epitomized these sentiments when he stated that the home was, first and foremost, a place where family members could grow toward exaltation together.[50]

The influence of righteous parents and a gospel-centered home is extolled by church leaders as the best way to protect children from falling into transgression. Women should remove themselves from the labor force so that they can watch over their children; men should provide for the family and preside over the home with the priesthood.[51] In such a home, it is promised, children will not depart from the teachings of the gospel.

Ninth church president David O. McKay is perhaps the church's best known advocate of the traditional, nuclear family.[52] In a conference talk that has become a classic in Mormon circles he said:

> No other success can compensate for failure in the home. The poorest shack in which love prevails over a united family is of greater value to God and future humanity than any other riches. In such a home God can work miracles and will work miracles.[53]

The sentence that begins the foregoing quote is a common Mormon maxim. The closing sentence, a puzzle for many pious families. The fact that having a homosexual son or daughter is not related to family religiousness has prompted many faithful Mormon families to ask, "Whence the miracles?" This is a dilemma for a church that teaches that being gay is learned and chosen. By the church's standard, having a gay child is most certainly "failure in the home" especially in light of the Biblical promise: "Train up a child in the way he should go: and when he is old, he will not depart from it."[54]

This scripture is fortified by the *Book of Mormon*, which states that church members who are steadfast in their beliefs will not "suffer [their] children ... that they transgress the laws of God."[55] Further, former prophet David O. McKay said: "Every child is, to a great degree, what he is because of the ever constant influence of home environment and the careful or neglectful training of parents."[56] And, finally, former church president Spencer W. Kimball writes: "Home life, proper teaching in the home, parental guidance and leadership are the panacea for the ailments of the world and its children. They are the cures for spiritual and emotional diseases and the remedy for its problems."[57]

For the most part, these "diseases" are believed to be sexual in nature, and Shepherd and Shepherd point out that the church's emphasis on stable, righteous families serves as a safeguard against sexual immorality.

> Traditional family life (in which the father is the head of the house, children respect and obey their parents, and parents set a proper example for their children) is legitimated as a divine institution which must be strengthened as a bulwark against the disintegrating forces and immoralities of the modern age. Sexual immorality is perceived as a prime evil to be guarded against.[58]

While having a homosexual son or daughter can present difficulties in any American family, the message of Mormonism exacerbates the problem. The Mormon prescription for strong, moral families implies that a home that raises a homosexual child is a home that is characterized by poor parenting.

Not surprisingly, Latter-day Saint parents of gay children suffer greatly when they discover a son or daughter's homosexuality. One mother writes:

> We have a homosexual son. (That has been the most difficult sentence for me to say.) ... They [my husband and son] had delayed telling me because they knew how much it would hurt me. They were right. ...The day he brought his temple clothing to me and said he could no longer be active [in the church] was a devastating day in all of our lives.[59]

Jan Cameron, the mother of a gay son and founder of the support group H.E.L.P. (Homosexual Education for Latter-day Saint Parents), writes: "we hurt as parents because we see our hopes and dreams diminish for that child—no mission, no temple marriage, no grandchildren, and worse yet, maybe no eternal family."[60] Informants corroborate, reporting that their families, especially their mothers, often blamed themselves for a having a homosexual son, and either shared in their child's guilt, or could not bring themselves to believe their son was gay. Jenkins recalls:

> I have talked at length with my own father about [my homosexuality]. It required a great amount from him. He is a good father, very loving, a bishop, high councilman, faithful and devoted to the church and his family. My mother, before she died, was never able to accept my homosexuality. On her deathbed she pleaded with me to marry.[61]

In addition to feeling unworthy, families with a homosexual son are often stigmatized by the ward. One informant said that "the folks in the ward started to murmur. They started to wonder what my mother had done that I turned gay." Another, describing a similar situation said, "That was the hardest for me. I felt like I had let my mother down because she blamed herself even though she had nothing to do with it."

LDS teachings about the relationship between church and family add an interesting wrinkle to the story of gay Mormons. The idea that "families are forever," is a stumbling block for gay people in the church, because they cannot enjoy true salvation without being married and raising a family of their own. But this doctrine also seems to be what shields them from excommunication in today's church, because cutting them off affects the quality of their parents' and siblings' salvation as well. However, sometimes homosexuality tears Mormon families apart in different ways. Many are deeply rent when a gay family member decides to leave the Mormon church.

The Choice to Leave Mormonism

The commitment to change from gay to straight, or the decision to remain celibate, are seen by many gay Mormons as the best ways to retain their church membership. But when these efforts fail, it sometimes leads them to finally withdrawal from the church. For most, the decision to leave Mormonism takes agonizing years, but many see it as the only way for them to enjoy sexual relationships, or live their lives as the person they really are.

Some gay Mormons, after years of intensive interviews and pressure from church leaders, begin to doubt their religion. "When I was trying as hard as I could, but ... I was still attracted to men, I started to think that maybe I wasn't the one with the problem. Slowly I started to doubt that this was really God's church." For others, the realization was more dramatic and sudden:

> One Sunday, two and one half years ago, I was teaching another gospel doctrine class when it dawned on me that I didn't believe anything I was saying. I had been absolutely repressing who I was. I had dated every single LDS woman in the region and felt no attraction to any of them. I sang in the [ward] choir, but the words meant nothing to me. ... I admitted to myself what I had always known deep inside. I asked for a release that Sunday and stopped attending church meetings. ... I essentially wanted nothing to do with an organization that had no use for me as a homosexual.[62]

Some reported that falling in love was the catalyst that led them to discard Mormonism. Ray, who had his name removed from church records, claims: "I found the meaning in [my lover] that I was looking for from the church." Thus, while they are given a healthy supply of "second chances" by today's church to change their orientation or reaffirm their celibacy, in most cases it is the gay man himself who eventually gives up on the church, and not the other way around. One writer claims:

> Many gays quietly slip away from the church with their faith in God usually intact, though somehow changed. Others stay, with the torturous knowledge that they can never participate fully and that the same brothers and sisters who profess to love everyone in the ward on Fast Sunday would feel a little differently if the truth were known.[63]

Those who do decide to stay in the church can choose between two basic strategies for harmonizing their sexual preference and the doctrines of Mormonism. First, they may accept the church's definition of homosexuality and its rules for the appropriate behavior of gay members. Those choosing this path attempt to keep the faith through celibacy, marriage, or by trying to change their sexual orientation. Alternatively, they may reject the church's definition and rules by attempting to reform the church through activism, either while living celibate or while living a gay lifestyle and hiding from the church. Those who choose to work within the church's guidelines are examined in chapter five. Those who seek a change in the church and who walk the tightrope between openly gay and actively Mormon are discussed in chapter six.

Notes

1. Joel W. Wells and William B. Kline, "Self-disclosure of Homosexual Orientation" *Journal of Social Psychology* 127 (1987): 191–197.
2. For an example of this type of rhetoric, see Spencer W. Kimball, *President Kimball Speaks Out* (Salt Lake City: Deseret Book, 1981).
3. *For the Strength of Youth*, (Salt Lake City: Corporation of the President of the Church of Jesus Christ of Latter-day Saints, 1990). A pamphlet in the author's possession.
4. Kimball, *President Kimball Speaks Out*, 10.
5. Mormon high school students are encouraged to attend a daily scripture study class called "seminary," designed to balance their school work with religious education.
6. John Mitchell, "Let's Communicate" *Affinity* 14 no. 11, (1992): 2.
7. The stage metaphor and the strategy of memorizing a hymn to chase away evil "players" was originally suggested by apostle Boyd K. Packer. See Boyd K. Packer, *Teach Ye Diligently* (Salt Lake City: Deseret Book, 1979).
8. This *Book of Mormon* verse reads: "And if men come unto me I will show them their weakness. I give unto men weakness that they may be humble; and my grace is sufficient for all men that humble themselves before me; for if they humble themselves before me, and have faith in me, then I will make weak things become strong unto them."
9. See also Anonymous, "New Friends," *Dialogue: A Journal of Mormon Thought* 19 no. 1, (1986): 133.
10. Cloy Jenkins, *Prologue*, 1.
11. Schow, et al. *Peculiar People*, 9.
12. Kimball, *President Kimball Speaks Out*, 10.
13. Jenkins, *Prologue*, 14.
14. *Doctrine and Covenants* 58:43.
15. Kimball, *President Kimball Speaks Out*, 14.
16. Schow et al. *Peculiar People*, 109.
17. "Priesthood" in the Mormon church is defined differently than in most Christian denominations. In the LDS church, the priesthood is offered to all worthy males. Composed of various levels, the initial office in the priesthood is offered to boys at age 12.
18. Richard R. Troiden, "Homosexual Identity Development," *Journal of Adolescent Health Care* 9 (1980): 105–113.
19. Masako Ishii-Kuntz "Unconsummated Homosexual Inclinations: Evidence from a College Sample," *Sociology and Social Research* 74 (1990): 222–226.

20. Women also serve missions for the church, but their participation in the missionary program is voluntary. By contrast, young men are commanded to serve a mission. Spencer W. Kimball states: "The question is frequently asked: Should every young man fill a mission? And the answer has been given by the Lord. It is 'Yes.' Every young man should fill a mission." See Leonard Arrington and Davis Bitton, *The Mormon Experience* (Urbana, IL: University of Illinois Press, 1992), 302.
21. Gary Shepherd and Gordon Shepherd, *Mormon Passage: A Missionary Chronicle* (Urbana, IL: University of Illinois Press, 1998).
22. Especially dedicated and experienced missionaries are often given the opportunity to be "trainers," responsible for giving new missionaries just entering the mission field instruction on seeking and teaching converts.
23. *The Missionary's Handbook* (Salt Lake City: The Church of Jesus Christ of Latter-day Saints, 1973). An official LDS church publication. A copy is in the author's possession.
24. Prior to departing for the mission field, missionaries are assembled at the Mission Home, now called the Missionary Training Center. Here, new elders are given inspirational talks by church leaders and memorize scriptures and lessons that will aid them in their proselytizing.
25. Schow, et al., *Peculiar People*, 24–25.
26. Jenkins, *Prologue*, 1.
27. Anonymous, "New Friends," 137, recounts the story of an elder who became "involved with a companion." No informant to this study reported engaging in a sexual act with a companion. A few, however, mentioned that they had been involved, or nearly involved with other church members in the mission field. Schow, et al., *Peculiar People*, 197, report that "Gary," a gay Mormon acquaintance, was involved in "non-orgasmic genital caressing" with a companion.
28. Missions are presided over by a mission president, usually an older man whose life has been characterized by dedicated church service.
29. The surreptitious (but always subsequently discovered) mid-month transfer for homosexual inclinations is also detailed in John Bennion, "The Interview," *Dialogue: A Journal of Mormon Thought* 19, no. 1 (1985): 167.
30. Missions are divided into zones that are presided over by an experienced set of missionaries called "Zone leaders." In mission slang, zone leaders are often called "Z.L.'s." Zone leaders do a great deal of traveling, and since some zones are large, they often spend the night with other companionships in the zone.
31. Schow, et al., *Peculiar People*.
32. Edward Gibbon's classic *The Decline and Fall of the Roman Empire* (New York: Penguin Classics, 1985) postulates that one of the reasons for the downfall of Rome was gross moral decay, typified by homosexuality.
33. A paraphrase of Jesus' admonition to an adulterous woman in John 8:11: "Go, and sin no more."

34. There are two divisions of the Mormon priesthood, the Aaronic, or preparatory priesthood is generally held by boys ages 12–18. Their priesthood responsibilities are limited and they can perform only a few priesthood ordinances. Adult men in the church, provided they are found worthy, hold the higher, or Melchizedek priesthood.
35. Schow, et al., *Peculiar People*, 24.
36. Almost all modern LDS church buildings contain a basketball court, and most wards field basketball teams and participate in church basketball tournaments throughout the winter. Basketball is an inextricable part of the Mormon male experience, especially in Utah.
37. Anonymous, "New Friends," 32.
38. A former bishop told the researcher that one possible reason for this advice is that experts in human fertility often counsel men with low sperm count to wear boxer shorts instead of briefs, since sperm production must occur at temperatures lower than body temperature and briefs can hold the testes too close to the body, making them too warm. Low sperm count was believed by some church authorities, he claimed, to be a cause of homosexuality. Another church leader mentioned that he had been instructed to tell young men in his ward not to wear briefs because their tight fit promotes nocturnal erections and emissions.
39. Anonymous, "New Friends," 1.
40. Ibid., 32.
41. Jan R. Stout, "Sin and Sexuality," 29.
42. Schow, et al., *Peculiar People*, 28.
43. Ibid.
44. Loren Fay, "Who Will Help Us If We Don't Help Ourselves?" *Affinity* 15, no. 2 (1993): 3.
45. LDS Institute is the university counterpart to seminary. The church has institutes of religion adjacent to most large universities in the western U.S.
46. *Achieving a Celestial Marriage* (Salt Lake City: Corporation of the Church of Jesus Christ of Latter-day Saints, 1992), 20.
47. Gordon Shepherd and Gary Shepherd, *A Kingdom Transformed: Themes in the Development of Mormonism* (Salt Lake City: University of Utah Press, 1984), 85.
48. Jan Shipps, *Mormonism: The Story of a New Religious Tradition* (Urbana, IL: University of Illinois Press, 1985), 149.
49. William Sims Bainbridge "The Religious Ecology of Deviance" *American Sociological Review* 54 (1989): 288–295.
50. Richard O. Cowan, *The Church in the Twentieth Century* (Salt Lake City: Bookcraft, 1985).
51. Ibid.
52. Ibid.
53. *Conference Reports* (Salt Lake City: Corporation of the President of the Church of Jesus Christ of Latter-day Saints, October 1962), 78.
54. Proverbs 22:6.

55. Mosiah 14:4.
56. Cowan, *The Church in the 20th Century*, 319.
57. *Conference Reports*, April 1973, 130.
58. Shepherd and Gary Shepherd, *A Kingdom Transformed*, 86.
59. Anonymous, "Letting Free Agency Work" *Sunstone* 14, no. 3 (1990): 5.
60. Schow, et al., *Peculiar People*.
61. Jenkins, *Prologue*, 48.
62. *Affinity* 14, no. 3 (1992): 5.
63. Ann Bullock, "Loving, not Liberated" *Dialogue: A Journal of Mormon Thought* 20, no. 1 (1987): 9.

CHAPTER FIVE
Celibate, Married, and "Changed"

The LDS church presently defines homosexuality as a chosen and, for many, a changeable condition. It further expects that homosexuals who wish to remain in the church either change their sexual orientation, or, if this is not possible, live a celibate life without sexual expression of any kind. While mistakes or "slip ups" in the form of some limited sexual activity are tolerated to a certain degree, gay church members who do not show earnest remorse and recommit to living church standards when they confess these transgressions must either lie to church leaders in subsequent interviews, or suffer church disciplinary actions. It is an uncomfortable compromise, but it is one that many are willing to make. Those who charge that the church is unrealistic in its demands are told that the church simply does not condone sexual relationships outside of marriage in any form whatsoever. One bishop, typical of others, defends the church by asking:

> What about a woman that is unattractive and no one ever asks her to marry? Should the church say, "Oh well, because it is not your fault you can have sex with whomever you please." No! ... So it isn't just gay people. There are many who have to manage without sex for the period of their mortal lives. Lots of people have to live without sex. I would hope that a priesthood holder in the Lord's true church would have at least as much faith and ability to sacrifice for the gospel as a Catholic priest. They volunteer not to have sex! Surely someone with the Melchizedek priesthood can be as strong as that!

The decision to choose celibacy as a method for managing the contradictions inherent in being a gay Mormon seems to be associated with several factors. First, informants in this group are characterized by high levels of religious devotion, and tend to come from homes that are similarly devout. Second, those choosing this route tend to be born into the church, and are likely to reside in areas where the social influence of the church is strong, like Utah. Finally, those who choose celibacy are more likely than others to be young, probably because—as we shall see—their older counterparts were either excommunicated or encouraged to get married, which they did.

Nevertheless, while church leaders may tolerate celibate gay people, it is likely that the lay membership of the church, if they had a say, would not.[1] Stan Roberts reports that the Stake High Council in his San Francisco ward debated whether or not to kick gay members out of the church, and individual ward members confided in him that they thought that gay people should be excommunicated.[2] So, while abstaining gay Mormons are allowed to keep their church membership, they are admonished to divulge their sexual orientation to others on a "need to know" basis. Depending on the bishop's advice, this may even include members of the immediate family. Gay Mormons are also strongly advised to sever all ties with other gay people they might know, and to eschew cultivating new associations with other homosexuals. What this means that the lives of most celibate gay Mormons are solitary and lonely, with few social outings.

Sometimes the solitude becomes difficult. Walter confided to this researcher that he started volunteering at a homeless shelter, "Not because I care all that much, but because it gives me someone to talk to. They're about the only ones who don't judge me." David reports that the local talk radio station is his "best friend," and Harvey frequents a computer chat network where he swaps stories with "other misfits, losers, and computer nerds who don't have a life." One man even reported that he drove around the streets at night looking for hitchhikers, just so he would have another person to talk to. Jenkins, whose experience as a gay Mormon has brought him into contact with many celibate homosexuals, writes:

> Recommending to the homosexual that he abstain from the sexual expression of who he is has far-reaching consequences. It cuts him off from the only real possibility open to him to experience love. The more frightening fact is that it unquestionably condemns him to a life of loneliness which cannot and is not ministered to by any facet of the

church or society. No amount of temple going, priesthood meetings, home teaching or special interest activity will ease the loneliness. This can only be realized through a mature, loving intimacy. The men who I know who have followed the course of abstention have a conspicuous diminution of humanness in their lives. They are, for the most part, a mixture of flat, uninteresting, impoverished personalities with a conspicuous tenseness and anxiety that is never focused or constructively expended.[3]

Mormonism and Singleness

For some, this solitude is self-imposed because they cannot bear the stigma attached to them by their family and former friends. Seth is typical among many gay Mormons who say "it feels like I have a scarlet 'H' or something on my chest." They report that being celibate is a "catch 22": if they reveal their sexual orientation, they will be stigmatized for being gay, but if they successfully live a celibate lifestyle, when they pass a certain age, they suffer the onus of being single in a church that demands marriage from every member.

RESEARCHER: Do you have family in town?
INFORMANT: Yes.
RESEARCHER: Well why don't you visit with them?
INFORMANT: Because they always bug me about getting married. They ask me if I'm seeing somebody or they say "We can set you up with so and so." They never stop.
RESEARCHER: So they don't know you're gay?
INFORMANT: No. But I don't know what's worse, having homosexual problems or being 31 and single.

Indeed, many report that being single in a church where only married people earn exaltation creates a formidable double bind. Seth continues:

That's very hard, too. The only time you are with another human being having fun is in the context of church. And that's a time when every second you are reminded that you are gay. Because the church is all about getting married and you are not. People say things about you. I know how some handicapped people must feel. I find that I catch people consciously avoiding the subject of marriage—just like you might find yourself trying hard not to stare at a person with a handicap. ... I wish they would just come out and say, "So why aren't you married?" I know they're thinking it.

Marriage is the highest priority of most young Mormons in their twenties. The church teaches that the decision to marry should not be postponed for an education or to acquire additional savings.[4] Moreover, being single into one's thirties has certain unpleasant repercussions in the church. A content analysis of LDS church general authorities' statements about being single revealed that:

> Being married is one of the most important ideas within Mormon culture, emphasized almost to the exclusion of other states of being. Much like the moon that is visible only when reflecting the sun's light, mention of singleness occurs most frequently in articles and talks about marriage, most frequently coupled with exhortations to marry.[5]

Because men in Mormon culture are supposed to initiate courtship and propose marriage, they are often characterized as selfish and immature by church authorities if they are in their late twenties or early thirties and are not married. Harold B. Lee, eleventh president of the Mormon church, announced: "Brethren, we are not doing our duty as holders of the priesthood when we go beyond the marriageable age and withhold ourselves from an honorable marriage to these lovely women."[6] Thus, single men in the church are seen as shirking their priesthood duties if they are not actively seeking marriage. Raynes and Parsons continue:

> Even though singleness is equally "wrong" for men and women, there were clear gender differences in the attitude of authoritative statements. Women were gentle victims of man's selfishness. Thus, unmarried men need to "repent" of singleness as they would any other sin, and the chief means of persuasion was threats.[7]

Participants in this study who were living a celibate lifestyle into their thirties report that the stigma associated with being single in the church was a tremendous burden.

In order to facilitate marriage as quickly as possible for those who happen to be single or divorced (also an undesirable status in the church), the church sponsors "singles wards," where single people are removed from their home wards and come together for worship services with one another. These wards (or "meat markets" as one informant called them) also host a variety of social functions, such as dances and outings, which encourage single people to interact and date.

The entire structure of these wards is geared toward marriage, and exhortations to marry as soon as possible are delivered with great frequency from the pulpit.[8] Ironically, homosexual men in the church are instructed to attend these singles wards because they are, after all, single. Attrition by marriage in singles wards is rapid, and gay men report that as they become the "old bachelors" in the ward, they are submitted to ever increasing pressure to marry.

To alleviate some of this pressure, many gay men begin to date women. Sociologists note that homosexuals often have a number of techniques that allow them to "pass" as straight in situations where they do not want their sexual orientation discovered.[9] Dating was one such technique used by the gay men in this study. "[Dating] gave me an excuse," said one, "because I could say that I just hadn't found the right one yet." Many informants said that they had excellent experiences while dating, and valued the women they dated as friends. But, when the women being "courted" began to press for marriage or a serious relationship, things often turned sour. Particularly disastrous were encounters where dates began to ask for and give physical affection. One writer recalls:

> On the way home my date slid over in the seat and started kissing me again. At her apartment I made a concerted effort at nominal petting. I tried everything, including the old ploy of thinking of boys. It was awful. I found myself growing physically ill. ... What does a person do who knows the gospel is true, who believes fervently in marriage for time and all eternity, who sustains the president of the church as a prophet of God, and yet is so warped that even kissing a girl can be accomplished only by cheap and demeaning subterfuge?[10]

Other Aspects of a Celibate Lifestyle

In addition to the pressure that comes from being single in the church, many celibate Mormons report that they have difficulty resisting the temptation to engage in sexual activity. Most know where the local gay taverns and "pick-up points" are in their towns, and most admitted that they had, from time to time, entertained the thought of visiting such places. In defiance of church counsel, many seem to have other gay friends that they have encountered at singles wards or other places. Informants say that they sometimes become involved in necking and petting with these associates. Some regard this as unacceptable and work toward eradicating these indiscretions, but others feel that a kiss or embrace is an allowance or small indulgence that they can enjoy from time to time. Eric employs the logic of the "single standard of morality" on his own terms, and reasons:

> A boy can kiss his girlfriend and it's not a sin, so I feel like I can kiss [my friend] and it is not a sin. I know my bishop wouldn't feel that way, but I think that the Lord feels like if it isn't a sin heterosexually, then it's not a sin homosexually. I'll tell you though, it sometimes gets hard to stop, but I want to be worthy for my mission.

Overall, however, most of the celibate Mormons in this study held themselves to very strict standards, and viewed even kissing and touching as inappropriate, although most said that they would not feel the need to approach their bishop for such a minor offense.

For some, the pressures associated with being gay and LDS eventually lead them to seek professional counseling. Although they are cautioned not to seek counsel outside the church regarding their homosexuality, the tension they feel can often manifest itself in other ways—typically in the form of stress-related disorders, which prompt them to go to the doctor for help. Sometimes, astute clinicians are able to ascertain that celibacy is part of the problem, and is affecting their mental health. One man writes:

> Recently one of my gay friends who is active in the church was told by his doctor that his celibacy was a source of unhealthy stress in his life. ... A couple of years ago I began seeing a counselor due to job-related stress. Though I was able to avoid discussing both my religious beliefs and my sexual orientation for many months ... when these factors finally did surface, the therapist immediately identified celibacy as a contributing factor in my over-stressed life. He [pointed out] that to deny myself of even the possibility of a loving, caring primary relationship was damaging to my self image, as well as to my relationships with others. ... There is no doubt that such counsel is one of the bones of contention between "traditional" church values and the psychiatric profession.[11]

For the most part, celibate Mormons described themselves as generally unhappy and resigned to an "incomplete" life, although this is not the case for everyone in this group. One interesting finding is that while celibacy has its obvious drawbacks, informants usually noted that living in self-imposed solitude was good for their careers. Those who were students typically excelled, and those in the labor force were rising stars in their respective companies. Said one, "It's kind of like how when you go blind your ears improve. Same here. I guess if you can't do things and serve another person you serve yourself." Most seemed to accept their lot in life, believing that this is truly the way God would have them live. Writes one, "I never expect, nor do I desire the church to condone homosexual practices."[12]

Still, several of the informants living a celibate lifestyle admitted that they were uncertain how long they could endure the strains of solitude. One man said that he "hold[s] on only because I believe these are the very last days, and Christ will be coming soon—within a few years." Some go to great lengths to remove themselves from the very possibility of succumbing to temptation. One man, who solved the problem by moving to northern Manitoba, writes:

> For those of us who are homosexual and committed to the restored gospel, life can be difficult at times. … I have solved the problem by living and working in an area far from either an organized ward or temptation. It is a very lonely life, but it beats the alternatives. … I carry on in the hope that at some time in the future, not in this lifetime I suspect, all things will be made clear. In the meantime, I endure.[13]

Others wait patiently, hoping against hope that new revelation from God will direct the church toward greater tolerance of homosexuality, and homosexual behavior.

Interviews collected for this study show that many men initially adopt a celibate lifestyle. Most abandon it after a few years, however, claiming that the costs are simply too great. But some who accept the church's definition of homosexuality and its behavioral prescriptions for gay church members, see it as their only choice, and continue down this path.

Homosexual in a Heterosexual Marriage

Less than a decade ago, celibacy would not be the appropriate response for those wishing to play by the church's rules. Until quite recently, the ultimate church prescription for "curing" homosexuality was to advise the gay person to marry. Many accepted (and some still accept) this advice, and, like many non-LDS gay people, entered into heterosexual marriage. Several of the older respondents to this study are either married or divorced. Most stated that while they had reservations about getting married, they thought at the time that this was the right thing to do, and something that the Lord would want. A few thought that marriage would change their sexual orientation. Others were more pessimistic, but felt that they could manage a happy life and an acceptable marriage in spite of their homosexuality. Norman, for example, states that he feels good about his relationship with his wife of eight years, but has problems dealing with the fact that he still has not told her the whole truth about his sexual orientation.

Most of the married informants in the study said that they were discouraged from telling their fiancées that they were gay. Church authorities, they report, assured them that things would change after marriage, or insisted that there were no homosexual people, only homosexual behaviors, and thus there was nothing to tell. Because of the church's strict stance against premarital necking, petting, and intercourse, informants said that their fiancées and girlfriends did not think that the lack of physical affection in their relationships was out of the ordinary, and thus the facade was fairly easy to manage. "She just thought I was a pillar of willpower," said one.

Joshua, ignoring the advice of his bishop, told his intended bride about his homosexuality, but his candid admission did not postpone or cancel their wedding plans. He recalls:

> We wept, of course, but in the end we decided that—she decided that—we should marry. As I look back on it, I see that she was getting old, you know, old and unmarried by church standards, and she probably thought that I was the best she could do. She was a wonderful woman and everything, but I guess she wasn't a real catch by "straight" standards. She had a "sweet spirit."[14]

While being gay did not seem to disrupt the courtship of some informants, serious strain usually surfaced shortly after the wedding. Many reported that they had a difficult time maintaining sexual relations. Some even admitted that they had to fantasize about men in order to have sex with their wives—something that filled them with guilt.

This lack of interest on the part of gay husbands was often interpreted by wives as a sign that their husbands did not love them, or found them unattractive. Most gay husbands had difficulty assuaging these concerns without finally admitting their homosexuality. One man, whose marriage eventually ended in divorce, writes:

> The marriage had problems from the very beginning. I loved my wife very much, but my innermost desires remained one of physical attraction toward men and not her. During this time, in addition to much prayer, fasting, and working in the church, I spent my entire life savings on psychiatric help to "cure my problem" and to save our marriage. My wife did not know the exact nature of the problem, but she knew that there was a problem and also worked, prayed, and did all she could.[15]

Informants generally claim that they tried very hard to save their marriages and salvage some semblance of a sex life before finally disclosing to their spouse the nature of their problem. Those who had the means usually spent years in personal and marriage counseling, and most increased their level of activity in the church in the hope that God would see their devotion and fix their problems. The church often counsels couples who are having difficulty in their marriage to have children, and so many became fathers, hoping that children in the home would mend the relationship. Some were able to remain married for a number of years, but their homosexual feelings did not go away. A former bishop writes:

> Little did I know (or wish to acknowledge) that festering within me were hidden aspects of who I really am. I am gay … I have been married with children for twenty years. One son is serving a mission. Even though my wife is my best friend and companion, I have known since my teen years that I have had an attraction for males, although until recently these feelings were kept well hidden.[16]

Eventually most of the married men in this study had to come clean with their spouses. One man writes:

> Sitting in the counselor's waiting room a short time later, I contemplated my reasons for being there. For 25 years I had remained virtually silent about my homosexual feelings. Along the way I had served a mission,

> graduated from BYU, married in the temple, become the father of two children, and held a variety of church callings from nursery leader to young men's president. I had been a virgin until marriage and faithful to my wife ever since. Nevertheless, the homosexual thoughts had not stopped when the "appropriate" avenue of intimacy had opened through marriage, as I had thought they would.
>
> My private means of dealing with what I called "my cross to bear in life" was through prayer, fasting, and dedicated church service. As hard as I tried to suppress my gay thoughts and fantasies, nothing had completely eliminated them. Sometimes I felt successful for periods of time, but eventually, the feelings would return. The hope of finally finding a "cure" kept me from fleeing the waiting room.
>
> [In the course of therapy] I was invited to consider telling my wife of my homosexual feelings. At that point in my life, I would have found it easier to cut off my right arm than discuss this subject with my wife.[17]

Other men had similar stories, and recalled that their wives were deeply hurt when they finally disclosed the truth.

The subject of marriage to a homosexual in the LDS church rose to prominence in Mormon circles when poet Carol Lynn Pearson, whose inspirational works are widely read among Mormons, published her book, *Goodbye, I Love You*. This autobiographical book tells the story of Pearson's marriage—a marriage to a homosexual man who eventually divorces her, contracts AIDS, and dies. *Goodbye, I Love You* was an immediate best-seller in LDS bookstores, and two informants reported that after reading the book, their wives confronted them about their homosexuality. Gordon states:

> I knew that [my wife] picked up [*Goodbye, I Love You*] because she had her suspicions. I knew that when she finished reading it she would know. I mean the book talks about all of the things that her husband used to do that should have tipped her off. The book is what tipped my wife off. I guess it was a good thing, though, because she approached me in a kind way, but she knew.

Discovering Gordon's homosexuality did not cause his wife to divorce him. The LDS church discourages divorce, even when one of the spouses is gay. When a couple afflicted with this problem approaches their bishop for counseling, they will almost certainly hear that saving the marriage is of paramount importance. Nevertheless, when such marriages do end in divorce, the church takes pains to minimize the stigma experienced by the wife.[18]

Some who remain married may be postponing the inevitable, but a few seem to be able to make it work, and report no signs of abnormal marital strife. Richard, for example, reports high marital satisfaction. He claims that his marriage actually improved after he admitted his homosexuality. "At no time," he reports, "did either of us even use the word divorce." He says of his marriage:

> Well, it is better than a lot of marriages. I think that there are people with a lot bigger problems in their marriage. I mean, our marriage doesn't have a lot of sexual fireworks or anything like that, but it has quiet respect and a great friendship. I'd rather have a very little in the way of a sex life than have adultery. Since we live the commandments we have been able to keep our marriage. Marriage was not meant to be easy, but it was meant to last forever. In the resurrection we will be happy that we stayed married. I think my wife would say the same thing.

Although many have tried to place themselves in Richard's position, few can actually attain it.

We can never know how many gay men are presently married in the Mormon church. But however many there are, they must surely far outnumber those few who say they have changed their sexual orientation, and claim to be "former homosexuals."

The "Former" Homosexuals

This researcher was puzzled, fascinated, and challenged by those who claim to have changed their sexual orientation. Claiming to be "cured" of homosexuality is a common strategy of those who want to duck out from under church pressure and intensive bishop's interviews, and I had always supposed that the letters on file with LDS Social Services from the many who had "changed" through prayer and fasting were from just such people. But there seems to be a small but active group of men who claim to have changed from homosexual to heterosexual through, as one puts it, "prayer, faith, repentance, and endurance." Most of these men were encountered at a conference sponsored by an organization for gay Mormons seeking to change called the Evergreen

Foundation, although some came to my attention through gay friends who were trying, unsuccessfully, to change.

Raymond claims to have reversed his sexual orientation. He points to a powerful religious experience that occurred during a trip to the mountains to pray that changed him "from a gay man, into a worthy man." Raymond describes the experience and its outcome with great emotion:

INFORMANT: It was like my head was being opened up and this being was looking at me, at my soul. I felt like that even though I was unworthy I was loved. It was a powerful being, but I knew right off it was an angel. I had been praying and I was on my knees, and I didn't look up. Then I felt great peace and when I got up, I knew that I had changed.
RESEARCHER: Changed? From homosexual to heterosexual?
INFORMANT: Yeah. I just felt different. I know it's crazy and you don't believe me, but that's okay. I know what happened. After that I was never tempted about men again. Then two years later I met my wife.
RESEARCHER: You never thought about men after that?
INFORMANT: Well, I thought about them, but not sexually. You know? Like a normal man thinks about men, as buddies.
RESEARCHER: And you began to desire women?
INFORMANT: Yes, like a normal man desires women. So I think that gay people can change. They just don't know they can change. They haven't tried hard. This happened after I'd been trying for years without goofing up.
RESEARCHER: So you feel like you chose to be gay?
INFORMANT: No, I think I was born gay; I just chose to be straight.

Spencer notes that he was involved in homosexual activity and had several lovers, but when the guilt overcame him, he approached his bishop for counseling. Unlike Raymond, his "conversion" was a process, and rather than change from homosexual to heterosexual, he seems to have changed from homosexual to asexual.

INFORMANT: I began to change my life. I repented and left my gay friends. Sooner or later, the excitement that I had for men left me.
RESEARCHER: So you no longer desire to have sex with men?
INFORMANT: No.
RESEARCHER: Do you desire to have sex with women?
INFORMANT: I don't desire to have sex with anyone. But if I was going to have sex with someone, it would be my [future] wife.
RESEARCHER: So, did you once fantasize or think lustfully about men?
INFORMANT: Yes, oh all the time. I was gay all the way.

RESEARCHER: And now?
INFORMANT: Now I realize that the world is preoccupied with sex. There's more to it than sex.

Some of the "changed" admitted to reorienting their bisexuality toward heterosexuality, and one expressed a belief that men who "are totally gay may have to live celibate."

But men like Raymond challenge what the psychiatric literature says about the ability of gay people to change their sexual orientation. More striking still is Peter, who insisted, after an initial interview wherein he detected my skepticism, on being re-interviewed with his wife present so that I would not think he was lying. Peter states:

INFORMANT: Through time though, and with a counselor, I started to change. I saw a new counselor that was LDS. Then we moved back to Utah to be closer to the church. I had stepped out on [my wife] before, but soon I had no desire to.
RESEARCHER: Stepped out with men?
INFORMANT: Yeah, but then in a few years I started to warm up to making love with her. Now, it isn't the kind of love they show in the movies, it's a more emotional love.

Research on those who claim to have changed their sexual orientation is *terra incognita* for sociologists who study homosexuality. The exact nature of this change, and whether or not it endures, is an important topic for future research.

Consigned to Hell

Quite unlike those who have successfully changed, the last group of informants who accept the church's definition of homosexuality and its behavioral mandates are those who have either tried to change and couldn't, tried to live celibate and failed, or got married and were unable to remain faithful. (Some have tried all three.) In spite of these failures, they are men who strongly believe that the Mormon church is God's only true church. They may attend church with their wives on Sunday, but they have secret homosexual liaisons on other days of the week. They have long since given up hope of changing, and seem to be convinced that they are destined to inhabit the telestial kingdom—the LDS equivalent of hell.

Most men in this category say that while they desperately wish they could change their sexual orientation, develop the willpower to live celibate, or be faithful to their wives, they are resigned to the fact that they cannot. They report that the lure of easy sex at gay bars or local "pick-up points" is too much for them to resist. One, typical of many, confided to me that

> at first I used to say to myself, "Stop that now. You can't go into those places anymore." Then after a while I stopped kidding myself. I stopped mocking God with false repentance and I just decided to not worry about it anymore. If I'm going to be judged by God anyway, I may as well do as I please. I'm going to the same place anyway.

Another echoes these sentiments, "I had left BYU and the church, convinced that I was going to hell and may as well find some small pleasures along the way. My homosexuality was too shameful a thing to admit to my dearest friends, so I just disappeared without looking back."[19]

Gay Mormon (or former Mormon) men who believe they are destined for hell are easy to find in Salt Lake City's gay bars. While some eventually manage to break free of the church and assuage the guilt associated with their homosexuality, some—years after their last church meeting—still feel that they are only biding their time, waiting for God to condemn them.

Notes

1. In the course of researching this book, I had occasion to discuss its theme and content with scores faithful Latter-day Saints. Most were surprised to discover that celibate gay people could remain church members, and some commented that they believed such individuals, whether or not they had engaged in homosexual activity, should be excommunicated. Crapo notes that official church policies often vary considerably from "grass roots" ideas about how the church should be run. See Richley Crapo, "Grass-Roots Deviance from Official Doctrine: A Study of Latter-day Saint (Mormon) Folk Beliefs" *Journal for the Scientific Study of Religion* 26, no. 4 (1987): 465-485.
2. Roberts, "Pastoring the Farside," 13.
3. Cloy Jenkins, *Prologue*, 20.
4. *Achieving a Celestial Marriage*.
5. Raynes and Parsons, "Single Cursedness."

6. *Achieving a Celestial Marriage*, 100.
7. Raynes and Parsons, "Single Cursedness," 36.
8. Anonymous, "Solus" *Dialogue: A Journal of Mormon Thought* 10, no. 3 (1976): 32.
9. See Brekhus, *Peacocks, Chameleons, Centaurs*.
10. Anonymous, "Solus," 41.
11. *Affinity* 13, no. 11 (1991): 4.
12. Name Withheld, "Choking in the Dust," 6.
13. Raymond M. Beaumont, "A Very Lonely Life" *Dialogue: A Journal of Mormon Thought* 19, no. 1 (1986): 23.
14. "Sweet spirit" is a common euphemism for "unattractive" in Mormon circles. It is typically used to describe women who possess all of the desirable qualities in a mate, except physical beauty.
15. *After Marriage, What¿* (Los Angeles: *n.p.*, 1980). A handbook in the author's possession.
16. "A Former Bishop Comes Out" *Affinity* 14, no. 12 (1992): 2.
17. Steve Morris, "Growing Pains: The Familiar Path to Self-Discovery" *Affinity* 13, no. 10 (1991): 3.
18. An LDS marriage manual sheds light on the church's position: "Under the most perfect conditions there would be no divorce permitted except where sex sin was involved. In this day divorces are permitted in accordance with civil statutes, and divorced persons are free to marry again without the stain of immorality which under a higher system would attend such a course." See *Achieving a Celestial Marriage*, 85.
19. *Affinity* 13, no. 4 (1991): 1.

CHAPTER SIX
MORMONISM AND THE "NEW MORMON GAY"

Not all gay Mormons accept the church's definition of homosexuality. Many have rejected this notion completely, claiming that their homosexuality is nothing to be ashamed of, and is an integral part of their personality. For those who regard being gay as an acceptable condition, yet still wish to retain their membership in the LDS church, a great deal of rationalizing and harmonizing is needed to make the two work together. Gay church members must navigate significant social and theological hurdles in order to keep their membership intact. Reaching a comfortable compromise between Mormonism and homosexuality is difficult, but there are some gay Mormons who make the attempt. A few seem to have succeeded.

Rejecting the Church Definition of Homosexuality

Gay Mormons often begin to accept their homosexuality as a permanent part of their life when they realize that continued struggles to change their sexual orientation are futile. Knowing that their attempts at changing or living celibate meet or exceed the efforts that heterosexual Mormons must employ to effectively live their religion, these men begin to feel that perhaps God accepts them as they are. This awareness, many informants report, eased a great burden of guilt and fear. Lach writes:

> When it first entered my mind that homosexuality might be a good thing basically, and that perhaps God wanted me to be as I am, I regarded it as a Satanic prompting. Paradoxically, I was filled with peace, well-being, and

> a sense of tremendous relief. It was as if I had been born again. As often as I would ponder those thoughts, they would bring great spiritual joy. There could only be one source of the peace I was feeling. I had felt it before, and, on my mission I had taught others to recognize it. Was I not under obligation to follow the Spirit in the direction I was being led?[1]

In spite of their belief that God accepts them as they are—a heretical position according to Mormon church leaders—many who reach this conclusion retain a firm testimony of the truthfulness of the LDS church. Most have no desire to leave the organization. Indeed, many will do virtually anything to keep their membership intact—except continue to deny their sexual orientation. Again, Lach explains:

> My own interest in gay/lesbian spiritual liberation is more than academic. I am a Mormon, from a long line of Mormons, yet, I am also a homosexual. I have come to realize that I cannot cease being either. Thus, happiness depends upon my ability to reconcile these two facets of my nature.[2]

Informants who choose to accept their sexuality *and* be actively LDS are an interesting and heterogeneous lot. Most are urbanites, and most are better educated than their celibate or married counterparts. Many are college students who have found that living away from home gives them the freedom to finally express themselves as gay men, but that the teachings of Mormonism still provide religious meaning that the university cannot give them. A number of informants in this group were involved in campus gay groups, and this association seems to have instilled in them something that other gay Mormons do not possess: a desire to challenge and question the church about its stance on homosexuality. Infused with a spirit of activism, these individuals have formed organizations for gay Mormons and have dubbed themselves "the new Mormon gays." The general aim of these "new gays" is to persuade homosexual Mormons to leave the closet and work toward changing their church. Their goal is nothing short of full acceptance for gay people and the institutionalization and official sanction of at least some form of homosexual sexual expression within the church. While they are in the minority, they are vocal. Much of the written output cited in this book was penned by gay Mormons pushing for their cause. Although they recognize that they are against great odds and are but a fraction of the homosexuals within the church, they see their course of action as better than the alternatives:

> The new Mormon lesbian and gay is indeed a rare species at present. Though not at all in danger of extinction, the numbers remain few. So far, they are very much the exception among homosexual Mormons, most of whom seem to be the willing 'heirs' of a tradition which exacts the heavy toll of individual autonomy and personal identity in exchange for a rather dubious existence of societal respectability and security.[3]

The logic of the "new Mormon gays" is simple. Most Mormons, they reason, even those who are highly religious, do not believe *everything* the church teaches. The church's stance on homosexuality, they assert, is one of those things with which they take issue. They part company with most doubting Mormons, however, when they call for action and attempt to persuade the church to change. They further distance themselves from other "closet" doubters by attacking one of Mormonism's bedrock social and theological issues: the definition of appropriate sexual conduct for church members.

In terms of acceptance in the larger gay community, gay Mormons' association with a church that is seen by mainstream gay people as "homophobic" is viewed as ignorant and backward. As one gay man, himself a former Mormon, puts it: "Anyone who hasn't left the [Mormon] church completely, in my opinion, is still in the closet."

Thus, gay Mormons who are openly gay and actively Mormon seem to be marginalized—stuck between two incompatible communities. Their course of action is to speak out against the intolerance of *both* antagonistic groups—calling for the church to accept them as homosexuals, and calling for "mainstream" gays to accept them as Mormons.

> Many of us, as Latter-day Saints, do not agree 100 percent with everything that the gay movement does or says. Likewise, we do not agree 100 percent with everything that the church says or does in regard to homosexuality. We are in a very delicate position: when we express our love of the Gospel and our Mormon faith and heritage, we run the risk of disapproval by our lesbian and gay sisters and brothers in "our" community; when we affirm our instinctive gay nature, we run the risk of swift excommunication from "our" church. The easy thing to do, then, is to just remain invisible and live a double life. But is that the honest thing to do? Does it help others? Does it help you?[4]

There is no doubt that the "new Mormon gays" are becoming increasingly visible within the church. They have also lobbied energetically for their cause, producing web sites and publishing articles and letters in the media outlets that cater to liberal Mormons and the LDS intelligentsia. A stern backlash to their movement has been evident. Orson Scott Card, a Mormon and well-known science fiction novelist, blasted gay Mormon activists in a *Sunstone* article, saying:

> One thing is certain: one cannot serve two masters. And when one's life is given over to one community that demands utter allegiance, it cannot be given to another. The LDS church is one such community. The homosexual community seems to be another. And when I read the statements of those who claim to be both LDS and homosexual, trying to persuade the former to cease making their membership contingent upon abandoning the latter, I wonder if they realize that the price of such "tolerance" would be, in the long run, the destruction of the church.[5]

According to sociologists Roof and McKinney most members of the LDS church would agree with Card. They note that Mormons compare favorably with even the most conservative Protestant groups in their condemnation of homosexuality, reporting that only 15 percent of Mormons agree with the statement "Homosexuality is not always wrong."[6]

But, in spite of this, the "new Mormon gays" have their supporters. Several articles in *Sunstone* and *Dialogue* have been written by heterosexual Mormons in support of gay church members. And certain presentations by heterosexual church members calling for increased tolerance have found their way into various symposia for Mormon scholarship and culture. Schow, a heterosexual, lobbying for some sort of sanctioned homosexual expression within the church, writes:

> Would Jesus find homosexual expression sinful on the grounds that sexual intimacy outside of marriage is forbidden? I doubt he would look at the matter that simplistically. The God-man who said that 'the Sabbath is made for man, not man for the Sabbath' would probably say something similar about marriage.[7]

Gay Mormons who want acceptance from the church have similar points to make. They make arguments and appeals to logic to try and convince others, as well as themselves, that homosexual relationships can be consistent with the teachings of the LDS church. For the most part, their rationalizations are rejected by the average Mormon, but liberal church members and gay Mormons who have not yet left the closet sometimes take heed. For the most part, their arguments seem to fit loosely into three broad categories, considered below.

Harmonizing Mormonism and Homosexuality

The first and most common argument used by gay Mormons pushing the church for change involves their generally held belief that homosexuality is an ineluctable part of their being. Since homosexuality is not a product of socialization, they reason, the church should not prohibit all forms of homosexual expression, because no one is foreordained to evil.[8] This reasoning turns one of the church's arguments against homosexuality on its head, namely, that because people are not foreordained to evil, homosexuality must be chosen. One informant, an astute student of Mormon scriptures remarked: "The *Book of Mormon* says that the Spirit is given to every man to know good from evil. I've known that I was gay since I was a little boy, but never felt it was evil—someone who has never been gay said it was."

The second argument states simply that prohibitions against homosexuality do not have the force of scripture or divine revelation behind them, and they are therefore valid only as the opinions of the individuals expressing them, even if that individual is an apostle or prophet. Gay Mormons point to the unique LDS doctrine of continuing revelation as evidence that these prohibitions reflect policy decisions made by church bureaucrats, rather than the will of God.

The church teaches that the president of the church and his apostles receive continuing inspiration and revelation from God. In the early days of Mormonism, church founder Joseph Smith wrote down the revelations that he received and compiled them into a book of scripture called the *Doctrine and Covenants*. As the church grew from a small movement governed by the charismatic authority of its founder to a larger one characterized by bureaucratic authority, this practice changed. Although modern apostles and prophets claim to receive revelation and inspiration, these revelations are no longer canonized like the writings of Joseph Smith.[9] This leaves open to interpretation just exactly which statements are binding on the church, which pronouncements have the authority of scripture, how much of what apostles and prophets say is their own opinion, and how much is the word of the Lord. For example, although individual prophets and apostles have spoken out vehemently against the theory of evolution, there is no official church statement that constitutes a divine directive on the subject. Theoretically, LDS church members may believe in evolution if they so choose, and some do. Church leaders have also spoken out against interracial marriage from time to time, but church members are, and always have been, free to marry anyone they desire without endangering their church membership.[10]

Gay Mormons point out that, like evolution and interracial marriage, there is no existing revelation about the nature of homosexuality, nor one concerning homosexual relations either. They argue that the speeches of apostles and prophets condemning homosexuality, because they are not presented as *revelation,* are merely the opinions and personal beliefs of those individuals expressing them. Indeed, in the entire corpus of Mormon scripture, excluding the Bible, same-sex relationships are not mentioned once. Noting this, one gay man writes:

> As [most Mormons] see it, the Lord by means of his prophets has repeatedly condemned homosexuality. But has He? Where are these prophetic denunciations so often cited by the opponents of same-sexuality? They are not found in the *Book of Mormon*, the *Doctrine and Covenants*, or the *Pearl of Great Price*—an astonishing omission given the alleged gravity of the sin. ... Mormon prophets have not condemned homosexuality on the strength of prophetic authority. ... Not even statements from the First Presidency which have appeared in various editions of the bishop's handbook can make the claim of [being revelation] since they represent an arbitration of policy, not doctrine.[11]

While it is true that the church does not have a doctrine of homosexuality, bishops point out that the church does have clear-cut doctrines that spell out what types of sexual expression are appropriate and in what context. Further, the *Doctrine and Covenants* contains an interesting phrase, used commonly by the LDS faithful, that ensures the prophet near infallibility when speaking on matters of faith. Fourth president of the church Wilford Woodruff, in a canonized declaration, assured the members of the church that "the Lord will never permit me or any other man who stands as president of this church to lead you astray."[12] This declaration seems to seriously injure the argument that homosexuality should be acceptable within Mormonism because it is not prohibited by revelation. The declaration is official, it is scripture, and it is widely known and quoted in the church. Still, this declaration is sufficiently broad and vague to allow one gay Mormon to feel comfortable remaining in the church by saying, "I have come to the conclusion that the only true revelation for guiding my life is personal revelation."[13]

Gay Mormons skirt the issue of Biblical verses that condemn homosexuality by referring to Protestant theologians and scholars who argue that these verses condemn homosexuality in the context of prostitution, rape, and idolatry, but do not prohibit homosexuality, *per se*. Lach, in a pamphlet for gay Mormons entitled *Homosexuality and Scripture from a Latter-day Saint Perspective*, performs a fairly complex analysis of these verses, attempting to harmonize them with Mormon doctrine. The success of his efforts, of course, depends on the reader.[14] Many gay Mormons, however, are satisfied with his response.

Mel Barber's article, "David Loved Jonathan: an Analysis of First Samuel 18-20" argues that homosexuality is actually condoned by the Bible by interpreting the famous friendship of King David and Jonathan as a homosexual relationship. Barber writes:

> As they secretly meet for the last time, David falls to the ground and 'they kiss one another' not just for a few moments, but 'until David exceeded' (I Samuel 20:41). To exceed means to pass or surpass, or in this case, to pass out with emotion. Now if that's 'friendship' or fellowship or brotherly love, I am certain that there are a few of us who could use a few more friends![15]

While these attempts to harmonize the Bible with homosexuality are interesting and no doubt helpful to some, most Mormons do not feel threatened by Biblical verses that contradict their beliefs anyway. For Mormons, the Bible, while inspired, is filled with errors and is an inferior work of scripture compared to the *Book of Mormon* and *Doctrine and Covenants*.[16] Mormon scripture states that the Bible is the word of God only "as far as it is translated correctly."[17] When presented with a contradiction between Mormon belief and the Bible, Mormons, gay or otherwise, are likely to refer to this Article of Faith in their defense.

Gay Mormons also point out that the founder of Mormonism, Joseph Smith, never mentioned homosexuality in any of his speeches or personal writings. In fact, a curious quote from Smith's diary was pointed out to this researcher by a gay Mormon who was very well versed in LDS church history. In the entry for April 16, 1843, Smith writes: "It is pleasing for friends to lie down together locked in the arms of love to sleep, and awake locked in each others embrace and renew their conversation."[18] Upon reading the quote to me, the informant remarked:

> Now I know that there is nothing sexual about that, but does that sound like something that a homophobic person would say? If homosexuality was such a sin, would a prophet who saw the face of God say a thing like that? Can you imagine [the president of the LDS church] saying something like that? What has happened to this church?

This last sentence exemplifies the third argument used by gay Mormons to harmonize their sexual preference and their religious beliefs. It is the claim that church leaders have fallen into apostasy. Evidence for this falling away, they assert, is the church's systematic discrimination against gays and women, something that the Lord would never condone. Several gay Mormons have blasted the church leadership on these grounds, stating that they believe that the prophets and apostles are not receptive to God's will, no longer receive revelation from God, and are abusing their priesthood power:

> I believe that Heavenly Father is disappointed in the leaders of the church for not bringing their misunderstanding of the sexuality of his gay children to him instead of leaning unto their own understanding.[19] I believe Heavenly Father is displeased with church leaders who seek to put words in his mouth by presenting their opinions as inspired truth. Only when they say "thus saith the Lord," is it scripture. Otherwise they speak as men.[20]

Another writes:

> Nevertheless, in the midst of admitted ignorance on the subject, church leaders continue to claim definitive answers to the questions about homosexuality, to rule arbitrarily on membership, and to demand blind obedience. Could such action be categorized as "unrighteous dominion," or an attempt to exercise 'control or dominion or compulsion upon the souls (and minds) of the children of men?'[21] I think that there is no doubt

that such actions are properly (and quite frankly charitably) so categorized.

We have learned from our own experience and long church service that what the church tells us about homosexuality is not true. Homosexuality is not learned and acquired; it is not something chosen. Prayer, church service, fasting, counseling, marriage, confession, shock therapy, excommunication, incarceration, and suicide do not solve or change the homosexual. Being raised a Mormon always exacerbates the psychological dilemma, because of the untruths that the church teaches.[22]

Some gay activists within the church see hope for their condition. Some say that these problems can be set right if gay Mormons play their cards right. They point out that the church is constantly changing, and is usually responsive to external pressures. Sometimes this is true. Threats from the federal government stopped the church from practicing polygamy, external pressure from civil rights groups was instrumental in pushing the church to allow people of African descent to hold the priesthood in 1978, and the women's movement seems to be moving the church toward greater recognition of women.[23] Thus, gay Mormon activists may have a point, and responsible activism, they argue, is the only way to bring about the kind of change and tolerance they desire.

Of course, this strategy is sedition, and engaging in such activism is grounds for excommunication. In spite of this, one letter writer to *Sunstone* writes:

As for the appeal to contemporary authority, it is, of course, the same sort of authority which once pronounced plural marriage the path to exaltation, but then later the sure road to apostasy; once explained black people as genetically separate because spiritually inferior, then later perhaps as equal but definitely separate, and finally mercifully as neither. It is an authority that until recently felt altogether comfortable with the notion that men are directly answerable to God while women, on the other hand, are directly answerable to men. Now, it seems, authority is no longer so comfortable. Oh, how times and the "timeless" change. And I for one am happy to see these awkward amendments to the "forever fixed, unchanging and eternal" pretensions in our rhetoric.[24]

Arguments against the church's stand on homosexuality and what one informant calls "respectful militarism" are the chief tools used to combat the ideological and theological contradictions that face gay

Mormons. But those who reject the church's definition of homosexuality must also negotiate a perilous social situation within the church as well. Dissension and protest are seen as sure signs of apostasy within the LDS church, and those who speak out often do so at the expense of their membership.

Maintaining their church membership is of considerable concern to many gay Mormons, and those that choose a gay lifestyle spend a great deal of time ducking the church and hiding their activities from church leaders. Many, because of the softening attitudes toward gay people in the larger society, are completely out of the closet, except to ward leaders and church contacts—the complete reverse of those who adhere to a celibate lifestyle.

Some allow their church activity to slip, or they travel from ward to ward with friends to avoid having to face a bishop's interview.

> We're the queer circuit riders. I try to go every week, but its a different place every week. My lover and I certainly can't live apart, but we know that if we're found out we'll have to go to a church court. He says he won't lie to the bishop, so we're the queer circuit riders. I don't want to get X'ed.[25] I don't want to lose the priesthood.

In spite of their open lifestyle and belief that the church is wrong in its condemnation of homosexuals, many who live an active gay lifestyle still shiver at the thought of excommunication. Many still believe that the true priesthood is to be found only within the church, and many still accept the *Book of Mormon* and the story of Joseph Smith. Roger, who has lived with a lover for three years, typifies the feelings of gay Mormons who would likely face church court if they were discovered:

> **RESEARCHER:** So are you really a member if the only thing stopping you from being X'ed is the fact that your bishop doesn't know you have a lover?
> **INFORMANT:** I don't think the bishop would be acting in the name of God if he X'ed me. No one has the authority to take my membership away but God.
> **RESEARCHER:** So why do you care if he knows you have a partner?
> **INFORMANT:** I don't know, I guess I shouldn't. I just figure that what he don't know won't hurt him, and it won't hurt me either. I'd feel—I don't know—naked if I got X'ed.

Thus, the fact that these gay Mormons engage in sexual activity does not necessarily diminish the strength of their personal beliefs. Many who have not attended church in years remain devout believers. One informant, from Washington D.C., mentioned that he had gone deeply into debt so that he could attend the University of Utah, where he hoped he could find a gay Mormon partner.

It is interesting to note that a number of informants who have rejected the church's standards for appropriate sexual behavior have nevertheless internalized the Mormon norm of endogamy. The newsletter of Affirmation, the largest, best organized support group for gay Mormons, regularly features personal ads where members can contact one another and develop relationships. Some ads even request that potential callers be returned missionaries. Match-making is a major function of Affirmation. Writes one member, "I don't come to Affirmation so much for the support, although I do get a lot of it. Mostly I like the people and the friends I've made. I really want to meet an LDS man and make a life with him."[26]

The tendency toward endogamy among these men is sometimes very strong. Some have even ended relationships that they felt were very rewarding and promising because their lover was of a different faith. One man writes, "While in Idaho I met a young man in the army and we became seriously involved. As much as I liked him, we eventually broke up because he wouldn't convert to Mormonism."[27]

Facing Church Court

All of this activity, of course, is of great concern to the LDS church. Although the church does not hunt down sexually active gay members to excommunicate them, when such a person comes to the attention of the bishop, the church will summon the member to a meeting with ecclesiastical leaders. As was mentioned earlier, those that show remorse for their actions, agree to repent, either move their lover out or move out themselves, and submit to the inevitable battery of interviews that are sure to follow such a meeting are usually spared the process of a formal church court. For those that show no remorse or who refuse to end their relationships, their removal from the church is a foregone conclusion. In a pamphlet for those facing excommunication, Affirmation leaders acknowledge: "If you are a homosexual and admit it, when you are called to a court you will be excommunicated; unless you decide to repent on the church's terms. You may avoid excommunication for a while, if you decide to lie to the court."[28] In fact, some do lie to the court, but in such cases the church is likely to follow up and discover that the gay person has given false information.

For many homosexual Mormons, facing a church court is very stressful. The thought of being cut off from the church, even for one whose membership has been marginalized by a homosexual relationship, is often difficult to bear. But some, like those who do not sustain the church president because of his stand on homosexuality, simply state that no one on earth has the right to excommunicate them from God's church. They vigorously deny the church court's authority, calling the action "unrighteous dominion" or an abuse of priesthood power. Some reason that membership in a church that has fallen away is not necessary for salvation and that excommunication does not remove one's priesthood or revoke one's temple blessings. Axelson and Mortensen, both excommunicated Mormons, write:

> Remember: your soul is NOT on trial; only your membership in the temporal church. They cannot take away your salvation, your testimony, your faith, your life or your God. They can only take what you let them. They will tell you that they are taking everything. There are many who have gone through this process before. They survive. They prosper. They succeed.[29]

They further reason:

> In reality, [excommunication] only means that your membership on Church records has been lifted and the exercise of priesthood authority no longer has the sanction of the church. The church cannot remove one's priesthood or the ordinances performed by it. It is interesting to note that when you come back into the church after excommunication ... your priesthood and temple ordinances are 'restored' by the laying on of hands. What this really means is that they never took them away in the first place. They are merely restoring the recognition and sanction of the church.[30]

Many excommunicated homosexual Mormons continue their lives after church court as if nothing ever happened. They attend church meetings in other wards when they desire, they read the *Book of Mormon*, and some even attend institute classes. Many search dutifully for a Mormon man. While most recall that they were deeply troubled and fearful about being called to church court, they seem to report that the experience was not as bad as they had expected. "I left feeling pretty much the same," said one, "I still feel the Spirit. It wasn't the end of the world." All of the excommunicated members in this sample indicated to the researcher that they still believed strongly in Mormon doctrine and the power of the priesthood, and expressed a firm desire to rejoin the church if and when things change.

Some gay Mormons, far from fearing excommunication, actually volunteer to be removed from church membership rolls. Michael explains:

> It is my form of protest. The scripture states that if you use your priesthood authority in a way that God would not approve of, then your priesthood power is null and void. I volunteered for church court because I wanted to protest. It was my form of protest telling the church that I am gay and there is nothing wrong with me. I am worthy of the temple and my partner and I should be allowed inside to be together forever. I have been excommunicated by the church, but not by God because those men did not have the authority to excommunicate me.

Many who voluntarily withdraw from the church remain interested in maintaining ties to the Mormon church through social interaction with other gay Mormons, and through church attendance or participation in other church functions. Most, like those who were removed from the church against their will, say that they "look forward to the day I can be accepted as God made me. When that happens I will be the first in line to be rebaptized. I know that the gospel is true, when the church is true again I'll be back."

The Conservative Reformers

Not all gay Mormons who would like to see the church change its position are so critical. Many are more soft-spoken in their rhetoric and tame in their behavior, but are just as firm in their resolve. There are those who reject the church's definition of homosexuality, but nevertheless feel that the best course of action to reform the church is to work *within* the church to change it. Firmly committed to the idea that homosexual relationships should be countenanced by God and the church, they feel that the best way to bring about the acceptance of such relationships is to remain celibate—speaking, but not acting, against the church. Such members are "out of the closet" even in church circles, but their lives are characterized by personal worthiness and a commitment to church service. They take every opportunity, however, to admit that they are gay, that God made them that way, and that they look forward to the time when the church will accept them as they are. One man writes:

> What could they do to me—stone me? For the first time in my life I realized that being gay and being Mormon didn't have to be mutually exclusive. The "contract" between me and the church was simple, I reasoned: I was expected to refrain from sex, but not from admitting my homosexuality.[31]

"Lead by example" seems to be the motto for those in this camp. They believe that by living the gospel to the letter, but insisting that homosexual expression should not be forbidden by the church, they will be able to show LDS leaders that they are worthy members and perhaps bring about change. "I feel working within the church will be more effective," one explains, "that's how blacks got the priesthood—not from confrontation."[32] Another, writing in Affirmation's monthly newsletter asserts:

> We can show people [that] even though we are gay, we can still have high standards and beliefs. Gay people can find the right mate and live together for eternity too! I am proud to be a member of the true church and a member of Affirmation, too! Let's show the church that we can be some of their best members.[33]

Often, those who choose this route are appalled and dismayed at the "promiscuity" of their more liberal counterparts. One informant confided to the researcher, perhaps naively, that "if all gays would play by the rules and stay morally clean, we might be accepted in the church by now." These sentiments are expressed more cogently by Postelwaite, who writes:

> The Gospel is still binding on us. We are still responsible for the light we have been given. The gospel is still the way to bring happiness into our lives and the only way to make it back to our Heavenly Father. Let us not

> use our sexuality as a cop-out to what we know is right. Because we love someone of the same sex is no reason to stop praying to our Heavenly Father, who loves us and wants to help us, or to ignore the blessings of the gospel in our lives and the happiness only it can bring.[34]

Thus, while waiting for a change in church doctrine and policy, these members are content to live celibate or at least severely restrict their sexual activity, all while asserting that homosexuality can be consistent with LDS teachings. Most seem to have unrealistic expectations about how much influence they can actually bring to bear on the church. And almost all are shocked and bewildered when they discover that they, in spite of their "moral cleanliness," have been summoned for a church court or disciplinary meeting with the bishop.

Most homosexual Mormons do not realize that in addition to their sexual behavior, the church is interested in their associations and in the beliefs that they publicly espouse as well. Just as feminists can face church disciplinary action for being actively pro-choice or supporting feminist causes that the church deems radical or dangerous, openly associating with other homosexuals and expressing a belief that contradicts church doctrine is grounds for church discipline. Axelson and Mortensen point out:

> Directives from the church indicate that to be excommunicated one must be guilty of homosexual acts; just being a homosexual or having homosexual thoughts or feelings is not sufficient. But most often church authorities use 'unChristian-like conduct' as the grounds for excommunicating homosexuals and consequently need not prove any act. Of course, from the list, other possibilities could be used but 'unChristian-like conduct' is the most common and the least difficult to prove.[35]

This researcher found that "apostasy" was the most commonly used excuse to disfellowship or sometimes even excommunicate a gay Latter-day Saint who had had no serious sexual contacts with other men. Again, when summoned by the church, individuals were given a chance to recant and agree to repent on the church's terms. Those who refused or did not show remorse were usually officially censured.

Among those whose actions did not merit a church court, many were still asked to relinquish their temple recommend.[36] During temple recommend interviews, potential temple goers are asked if they knowingly associate or sympathize with any apostate group or apostate cause. An answer in the affirmative is sufficient to warrant the suspension of a recommend. Thus, it is difficult for any gay Mormon who openly rejects the LDS church's definition of homosexuality to function as a church member in full faith and fellowship.

Affirmation

More often than not, when the temple recommend of a gay Mormon is revoked for association with apostates, the apostate group in question is Affirmation. This group is the landing spot for many gay Mormons who want to push the church to change its stand on homosexuality. In its early years, gay Mormons report that Affirmation was a great source of support and information, helping many sort out the contradictions and pitfalls associated with being gay and LDS. While some informants gave Affirmation high marks, most said that the group is now wracked with internal dissent. Leadership changes are frequent, and disputes over the mission and purpose of the organization are sometimes acrimonious. The problems arise from the fact that Affirmation membership is split almost evenly into two rival camps. Camp one contains those who are heavily involved in the gay rights movement, are active in regional and national gay issues, and who subscribe to the methods of activism employed by certain high-profile gay groups. Many in this group have voluntarily chosen excommunication, or have been cut off from the church after their sexual behavior was uncovered by ward leaders.

Most of these gay Mormons say that they still believe in the church "deep down inside," but that they can have nothing to do with the organization until it changes its homophobic ways. For them, Affirmation meetings are mostly a chance to meet with others who have been down the same difficult path of being gay and being Mormon. It is a chance for them to swap "war stories" (many of which have found their way into this book.) Some even use the meetings as a place to pick up sexual contacts. One man states, "It's just that because they are Mormons or ex-Mormons we have more in common. I usually have a nice evening with men I meet here because we have a lot to discuss."

Camp two consists of those who want to move for reform from within the church, and who look to Affirmation more for support in harmonizing homosexuality and Mormonism than in providing social contacts. Members of this faction are often shocked at the liberal attitude toward sexuality of other Affirmation members. One pointed out that he was "stunned when [Affirmation leaders] handed out condoms at a retreat, but didn't open the meeting with prayer." They are similarly disapproving of the tactics that members of the more vocal faction use to attract the attention of the church. One writes:

> I would not like to see Affirmation members chained to the temple gates in protest. I think political activity should be handled in a socially acceptable manner. We should make ourselves known in the church—our numbers and strength—but I don't want to be a part of a renegade Mormon group. I think there is a midpoint where Affirmation can be positive, supportive, educational and a benefit to gay LDS members and, in a small way, good for the church.[37]

Like those in Thumma's study who left the predominantly gay Metropolitan Community Church to join a conservative gay evangelical group, conservative members of Affirmation feel that the group's more outspoken members are "putting gay before God."[38] "They don't act like Latter-day Saints," one remarked, "they have no testimony."

Things have been this way in Affirmation for over a decade. A survey of Affirmation's membership, published in the group's newsletter in the early 1990s, shows just how polarized the two camps were at this time, and how evenly divided the membership was between them. For example, 46 percent of those polled reported that their membership was intact, while 48 percent were excommunicated (voluntarily or otherwise) or disfellowshipped—a near even split. Church attendance was also polarized. Forty-four percent were regular or occasional church goers, while 54 percent rarely or never attended church. With regard to sexual activity, 24 percent were either celibate, or have sexual relations no more than yearly, while a full 66 percent reported sexual relations weekly or daily.[39]

Shortly after this membership survey was taken, divisions between the two camps came to a choleric head in a famous incident at the annual Affirmation retreat. The controversy centered, among other things, on the selection of a non-LDS keynote speaker. One man, upset by the choice of speaker and its implication, wrote a letter to Affirmation's newsletter expressing his displeasure:

> How can the [keynote speaker], a non LDS individual enlighten us [on the plight of gay Mormons]? I feel as though the general authorities had invited Oral Roberts or Billy Graham to offer the opening address at General Conference. ... As a returned missionary, I relate to the similar struggles experienced by other RMs—the long hours of fasting and prayer, soul searching, and family confrontations—but a non-Mormon just has no idea what we've gone through. My needs (and I'm sure my view is echoed by many others) would be much better met by hearing the personal stories of fellow RMs and how they've been able to integrate their sexuality with Mormonism.[40]

Tensions were high at the retreat, and many with a more conservative bent were angry at the way the conference was handled. "It was totally nondenominational," said one. "You would hardly have known that we were Mormon gays. It was like any other gay activity." Another remarked, "I don't feel my needs are being met as an *active* LDS person."[41]

Sensing that this dissension could spell the end of Affirmation, the group's leadership again changed hands in 1993. In an address to the members of Affirmation, executive director Marty Beaudet conceded, "The light at the end of Affirmation's tunnel has been dim recently, if not completely turned off." He added, however, with cautious optimism: "I would hope that the beginning of our term on the executive committee will have a brightening effect on it."[42] Nevertheless, Beaudet was resigned to the fact that repairing the rift between the two polarized camps was an impossibility, and instead opted for a "strength in diversity" theme saying, "If Affirmation has seemed to stagnate and struggle to grow in the past, it is not due to our differences, but our inability to understand and accept those differences."[43]

One of the leadership's biggest woes is the inability of the organization to retain members. A full 40 percent of Affirmation's membership choose not to renew every year, and the group's core membership is largely comprised of long-term members with little new blood. The reason for this, in spite of what each successive new leadership team might think, is not that the organization is necessarily being mishandled or that the polarization of members is the harbinger of inevitable extinction. It may be, rather, that Affirmation is most effective as a "halfway-house" for gay Mormons who are deciding whether to place their faith in the church's definition and prescription for homosexuality and homosexual behavior, or to part with the church once and for all and assume a more mainstream gay identity.

Those who are leaning toward an open, unencumbered gay lifestyle use Affirmation to wean themselves from the cultural and spiritual ties that continue to bind them to Mormonism. Once mere vestiges of these ties remain, they leave the church—though some still continue to have certain aspects of a Mormon upbringing still embedded within them.

> It [my decision to leave the church] still haunts me. My lover asked me the other day about something from the temple ceremony and I just couldn't [divulge the information]. I was afraid to say it.[44] It still sort of follows me around. I still can't decide what to do with all those experiences I had on my mission. It has made me very afraid of death.

In contrast, those who prefer the security of the church over the expression of their sexuality see for themselves that managing a homosexual lifestyle is probably not possible within the context of orthodox Mormonism, and turn their back on the mainstream gay experience to seek happiness within the confines of the church. Either way, both groups are, for the most part, destined to leave Affirmation. Either way, all gay Mormons must, at some point, choose whether they will follow the edicts of the prophets or embrace their sexuality. As one writer succinctly observes:

> There is much that is good and beautiful in LDS theology. Some people who recognize their homosexuality are willing to walk the mental tightrope to stay in the church while others can't. Either way, the decision is extremely painful—like cutting out a part of yourself.[45]

Notes

1. Lach, *Homosexuality and Scripture*, 35–36.
2. Ibid., 34.
3. See Cheever, "Self Help," 16. The use of the word "societal" here probably refers to Utah communities where the lines between church standards and community standards are blurry.
4. Mel Barber, "Invisible, But Not Alone" in *Affirmations: A Select Anthology of Writings for Gay and Lesbian Mormons*. (*n.p.*, 1985), 21.

5. Orson Scott Card, "The Hypocrites of Homosexuality" *Sunstone* 14, no. 1 (1990): 44.
6. Wade Clark Roof and William McKinney, *American Mainline Religion: It's Changing Shape and Future* (New Brunswick, NJ: Rutgers University Press, 1987).
7. Schow, et al. *Peculiar People*, 11.
8. For a discussion of the Mormon doctrine of foreordination and its implications for gay members, see chapter three.
9. With rare exception. The 1978 church decision to allow people of African descent to hold the priesthood was canonized and placed as an appendix to the *Doctrine and Covenants*. It was not, however, divided into verses or presented in "King James" English as were the revelations of Joseph Smith.
10. See Crapo, "Grass-Roots Deviance from Official Church Doctrine" for a complete discussion of the nature of official doctrine and its relationship to Mormon folk belief.
11. Lach, *Homosexuality and Scripture*, 3.
12. See "Official Declaration 1" in the *Doctrine and Covenants*.
13. Paul Mortensen, "Revelation: A Very Personal Communication" in *Affirmations: A Select Anthology of Writings for Gay and Lesbian Mormons*. (*n.p.*, 1985), 31.
14. Lach, *Homosexuality and Scripture.*
15. Mel Barber, "David Loved Jonathan: An Analysis of I Samuel 18–20" in *Affirmations: A Select Anthology of Writings for Gay and Lesbian Mormons*. (*n.p.*, 1985), 36.
16. Philip Barlow, *Mormons and the Bible: The Place of the Latter-day Saints in American Religion* (New York: Oxford University Press, 1991).
17. This assertion is Article of Faith 8 in the *Pearl of Great Price*.
18. Scott Faulring, *An American Prophet's Record: The Diaries and Journals of Joseph Smith* (Salt Lake City: Signature Books, 1987), 366.
19. A reference to Proverbs 3:5
20. Richard Postelwaite "Remember Who You Are" in *Affirmations: A Select Anthology of Writings for Gay and Lesbian Mormons*. (*n.p.*, 1985), 28.
21. This is a reference to *Doctrine and Covenants* 121:39, a famous Mormon scripture which states, "We have learned by sad experience that it is the nature and disposition of almost all men, as soon as they get a little authority, as they suppose, they will immediately begin to exercise unrighteous dominion."
22. Gordon Miller, "Open Letter to Members and Friends of Affirmation" in *Affirmations: A Select Anthology of Writings for Gay and Lesbian Mormons*. (*n.p.*, 1985), 45.
23. On polygyny see Richard S. Von Wagoner, *Mormon Polygamy: A History* (Salt Lake City: Signature Books, 1986). On Women's issues, see Maxine Hanks, *Women and Authority: Re-emerging Mormon Feminism* (Salt Lake City: Signature Books, 1992). On race issues, see Armand L. Mauss, *All Abraham's Children: Changing Mormon Conceptions of Race and Lineage* (Urbana, IL: University of Illinois Press, 2003).

24. Neal Chandler, "Give it a Rest" *Sunstone* 14, no. 5 (1990): 5.
25. "X'ed" is Mormon slang for excommunicated.
26. *Affinity* 13, no. 12 (1991): 6.
27. D. K. Johnsen, "Just One Breath" *Affinity* 13, no. 7 (1991): 3.
28. Robert T. Axelson and Paul Mortensen. *Excommunication: A Survival Manual for Gay and Lesbian Mormons* (*n.p.*), 11. Emphasis in original. This is a booklet published by Affirmation in the author's possession.
29. Ibid., 3. Emphasis in original.
30. Ibid., 12.
31. *Affinity* 13, no. 4 (1991): 1.
32. *Affinity* 13, no. 12 (1991): 6.
33. Ibid.
34. Postelwaite, "Remember Who You Are," 28.
35. Axelson and Mortensen, *Excommunication*, 7.
36. Entrance into the temple is strictly controlled. Only those screened by their bishops may enter. When one has been found worthy to enter the temple, a "temple recommend" is issued. The bishop or stake president, however, reserves the right to revoke this recommend if an individual is found unworthy in the course of subsequent interviews.
37. *Affinity* 13, no. 12 (1991): 6.
38. See Thumma, "Negotiating a Religious Identity."
39. *Affinity* 13, no. 12 (1991): 2–3.
40. Gary Gerwin, "Keynote Outsider" *Affinity* 13, no. 11 (1991): 2.
41. Rick Fernandez, "Mission Statement Survey Results" *Affinity* 14, no. 6 (1992): 2. Emphasis in original.
42. Marty Beaudet, "What you can Expect from the New Leadership" *Affinity* 15, no. 2 (1993): 1.
43. Ibid.
44. Members attending the LDS temple swear an oath never to reveal the particulars of the ceremony to others. Doing so constitutes grievous sin.
45. Bullock, "Loving, not Liberated," 9.

CHAPTER SEVEN
EPILOGUE

This book has focused on how gay individuals within the Mormon church must choose between two competing labels of homosexuality and the conflicting prescriptions for the appropriate behavior of people that are attached to these labels. The modern, high profile push for gay rights in America presents one label and one set of behavioral guidelines, inviting gay people to take pride in their sexual orientation, to disavow traditional attitudes which regard homosexuality as perverted and sinful, and to live openly and proudly as gay individuals. The influence of this message on gay people, including gay Mormons, is very powerful.

Conversely, the LDS church, a powerful force in the lives of most active church members, teaches that homosexuality is inferior to heterosexuality. It presents gay Mormons with a chance to achieve eternal salvation by either changing—through faith and devotion—from a homosexual to a heterosexual, or by living a celibate life with a promise of eternal rewards for this abstinence in the next life.

The rewards of the gay rights movement involve the here and now, the rewards offered by Mormonism involve the hereafter. Neither has much to give to the other realm. For gay *Mormons*, life without the teachings of the church is a life without the security of family and loved ones in heaven, and a knowledge that one must face the world without the power to act in God's name. For Mormon *gays,* life without the hope of a partner or appropriate sexual expression is often the prescription for a lonely and unfulfilled life. Each domain is diametrically opposed to the other, and each is, in its own way, an inextricable part of the life and worldview of the homosexual Mormon.

In the preceding chapters we have seen how some choose to leave the church in favor of an open, expressive homosexual lifestyle—the here and now. We have seen how some choose to abandon or repress their homosexuality in favor of the security of knowing that an eternal reward awaits beyond the grave. And, finally, we have also seen how some, unable to completely let go of either the temporal or the eternal, have tried to manage and balance the two together.

There is, however, one group that remains. Unable to reconcile homosexuality with Mormonism, and unable to compromise or give up either, an unknown, but significant number of gay Mormons choose to take their own lives. Emile Durkheim asserts that people who are no longer able to find meaning in society and who are unable to fit into social groups in meaningful ways suffer from what he calls a state of "anomie"—feelings of worthlessness and normlessness. Unable to find their place in the larger culture, the anomic may turn to suicide.[1]

As chapter four points out, suicidal thoughts are common among gay Mormons. These thoughts seem to reflect the marginal position—the anomie—of those inescapably tied to two incompatible labels. One LDS homosexual says:

> **INFORMANT:** I think about suicide because I can't see where I would fit in. I mean you can't be a Mormon and be gay, and you can't be gay and be a Mormon. I mean that's all I know.
> **RESEARCHER:** How often do you think about suicide?
> **INFORMANT:** Do you see this? [Lifts up bed skirt, reaches down, shuffles around in a box and reveals a pistol.]
> **RESEARCHER:** Whoa!
> **INFORMANT:** I think one day I'll probably use it.
> **RESEARCHER:** I think that maybe you should see somebody ...
> **INFORMANT:** [cutting off researcher] What are they going to tell me? Huh? Either don't be gay or don't be Mormon.

Sometimes, being faced with excommunication and losing the meaning and security provided by the church is the deciding factor that prompts a gay Mormon to commit suicide. An Affirmation publication reports, "We have no statistics to back this up, but we are certain that many people commit suicide rather than face the disgrace of excommunication."[2] One informant recalls his experience:

> When [my partner] got the letter [summoning] him to church court he cried for days. He said he could not live without the church. I was concerned about him, but I didn't think he was serious. He said we would have to break up. I thought he was depressed but that he would get over it. ... When I came home from work [several nights later] he had [asphyxiated himself in the car]. His note said that he didn't know what to do. That to die by suicide was better than to live without the church or me.

And a letter writer to *Dialogue* adds:

> My friend Steve was ... a gay Mormon. Entrapped by BYU security, he "voluntarily" underwent aversion therapy at BYU and was later pressed into marriage by a zealous stake president who claimed that prayer, laying on of hands, and "commitment" had cured him. It hadn't and a few years later Steve was sexually active with other men, estranged from his wife and children, and overwhelmed by guilt—the product of a good Mormon upbringing that had taught him to hate himself. Despairing, Steve turned to the church for help and was eventually excommunicated by a "court of love." Two weeks later he took his own life.[3]

The number of gay Mormons who choose suicide can never be known. But it is not surprising, given the stumbling blocks that are placed in their way regardless of which way they turn, that some do. The very fact that suicide is a viable option for those involved in the delicate balancing act between Mormonism and homosexuality lends credence to the idea, presented in the introduction to this book, that the meanings and labels attached to statuses by powerful social institutions are of great importance for those inhabiting those statuses. In some cases, as we have seen, meaning is more important than life itself.

Notes

1. Emile Durkheim, *Suicide* (New York: Free Press, 1966).
2. *After Marriage, What?*, 5.
3. Letter to the editor, *Dialogue: A Journal of Mormon Thought* 21, no. 1 (1988), 5.

Bibliography

Achieving a Celestial Marriage. Salt Lake City: Corporation of the Church of Jesus Christ of Latter-day Saints, 1992.

Affinity. The monthly newsletter of Affirmation. Copies are in the author's files.

Affirmation Charter. *n.p.*, 1990. The membership charter and constitution of Affirmation. A copy is in the author's files.

After Marriage, What? Los Angeles: *n.p.*, 1980. A booklet published by Affirmation. A copy is in the author's files.

Allen, Chris. "Conference on Changing Gay Orientation Stirs Controversy" *Sunstone* 14, no. 3 (1990): 62.

Almaguer, Thomas. "Chicano Men: A Cartography of Homosexual Identity and Behavior," *Differences* 3, no. 1 (1991): 75–100.

Anonymous. "New Friends," *Dialogue: A Journal of Mormon Thought* 19 no. 1 (1986): 133.

Anonymous. "Solus" *Dialogue: A Journal of Mormon Thought* 10, no. 3 (1976): 32.

Arrington, Leonard and Davis Bitton. *The Mormon Experience*, New York: Vintage Books, 1979.

Axelson, Robert T. and Paul Mortensen. *Excommunication: A Survival Manual for Gay and Lesbian Mormons*. *n.p*. A booklet in the author's possession.

Bainbridge, William Sims. "The Religious Ecology of Deviance" *American Sociological Review* 54 (1989): 288–295.

Barber, Mel. "David Loved Jonathan: An Analysis of First Samuel 18–20" in *Affirmations: A Select Anthology of Writings for Gay and Lesbian Mormons*. *n.p.*, 1985.

———. "Invisible, But Not Alone" in *Affirmations: A Select Anthology of Writings for Gay and Lesbian Mormons*. *n.p.*, 1985.

Barlow, Philip. *Mormons and the Bible: The Place of the Latter-day Saints in American Religion*, New York: Oxford University Press, 1991.

Beaudet, Marty. "Homophobic Rameuptoms" *Sunstone* 14, no. 3 (1990): 3.

———, Marty. "What you can Expect from the New Leadership" *Affinity* 15, no. 2 (1993): 1.

Beaumont, Raymond M. "A Very Lonely Life" *Dialogue: A Journal of Mormon Thought* 19, no. 1 (1986): 23.

Becker, Howard S. *Outsiders*. New York: The Free Press, 1963.

Bennion, John. "The Interview," *Dialogue: A Journal of Mormon Thought* 19, no. 1 (1985): 167.

Berger, Peter. *The Sacred Canopy: Elements of a Sociological Theory of Religion*. New York: Doubleday, 1969.

Brekhus, Wayne. *Peacocks, Chameleons, Centaurs: Gay Suburbia and the Grammar of Social Identity*. Chicago: University of Chicago Press, 2003.

Broderick, Carlford. *One Flesh, One Heart*, Salt Lake City: Deseret Book, 1986.

Brown, Victor L. *Fred's Story*, Sacramento, CA: HR Associates, 1985.

Bruce, F. F. *I and II Corinthians*. Grand Rapids, MI: Eerdmans, 1971.

Bullock, Ann. "Loving, not Liberated" *Dialogue, A Journal of Mormon Thought* 20, no. 1 (1987): 9.

Card, Orson Scott. "The Hypocrites of Homosexuality" *Sunstone* 14, no. 1 (1990): 44.

Chandler, Neal. "Give it a Rest" *Sunstone* 14, no. 5 (1990): 5.

Cheever, Grant. "Self Help" in *Affirmations: A Select Anthology of Writings for Gay and Lesbian Mormons*. *n.p.*, 1985.

Cloy Jenkins. *Prologue: An Examination of Mormon Attitudes Towards Homosexuality*. Provo, UT: Prometheus Enterprises, 1978.

Conference Reports. Salt Lake City: Corporation of the President of the Church of Jesus Christ of Latter-day Saints, October 1962.

Cowan, Richard O. *The Church in the Twentieth Century*. Salt Lake City: Bookcraft, 1985.

Crapo, Richley. "Grass-Roots Deviance from Official Doctrine: A Study of Latter-day Saint (Mormon) Folk Beliefs" *Journal for the Scientific Study of Religion* 26, no. 4 (1987): 465–485.

Denzin, Norman K. *The Research Act: A Theoretical Introduction to Sociological Methods*. Englewood Cliffs, NJ: Prentice Hall, 1989.

Doctrine and Covenants. Salt Lake City: The Church of Jesus Christ of Latter-day Saints, 1981.

Durkheim, Emile. *Suicide*, New York: Free Press, 1966.

England, Eugene. "Empathy Not Confusion" *Dialogue: A Journal of Mormon Thought* 20, no. 3 (1987): 6.

Ensign of the Church of Jesus Christ of Latter-day Saints. Salt Lake City: Corporation of the President of the Church of Jesus Christ of Latter-day Saints. A monthly magazine published by the LDS church.

Faulring, Scott. *An American Prophet's Record: The Diaries and Journals of Joseph Smith*, Salt Lake City: Signature Books, 1987.

Fay, Loren. "Who Will Help Us If We Don't Help Ourselves¿" *Affinity* 15, no. 2 (1993): 3.

Fernandez, Rick. "Mission Statement Survey Results" *Affinity* 14, no. 6 (1992): 2.

For the Strength of Youth. Salt Lake City: Corporation of the President of the Church of Jesus Christ of Latter-day Saints, 1990.

Gagnon, Robert A. J. *The Bible and Homosexual Practice: Texts and Hermeneutics*. Nashville, TN: Abingdon Press, 2002.

Gerth, H. H. and C. Wright Mills (eds). *From Max Weber: Essays in Sociology*. New York: Oxford University Press, 1947.

Gerwin, Gary. "Keynote Outsider" *Affinity* 13, no. 11 (1991): 2.

Gibbon, Edward. *The Decline and Fall of the Roman Empire*. New York: Penguin Classics, 1985.

Goffman, Erving. *Stigma: Notes on the Management of a Spoiled Identity*. Englewood Cliffs, NJ: Prentice Hall, 1963.

Hanks, Maxine. *Women and Authority: Re-emerging Mormon Feminism*, Salt Lake City: Signature Books, 1992.

Heaton, Tim B. "Four Characteristics of the Mormon Family: Contemporary Research on Chastity, Conjugality, Children and Chauvinism," *Dialogue: A Journal of Mormon Thought* 20, no. 2 (1987): 101–114.

Homosexuality. Salt Lake City: Corporation of the President of the Church of Jesus Christ of Latter-day Saints, 1981. A copy is in the author's files.

Hooker, Evelyn. "The Adjustment of the Male Overt Homosexual," *Journal of Projective Techniques* 21 (1957): 18–31.

Horwitz, Allan V., *Creating Mental Illness*. Chicago: University of Chicago Press, 2003.

Ishii-Kuntz, Masako. "Unconsummated Homosexual Inclinations: Evidence from a College Sample," *Sociology and Social Research* 74 (1990): 222–226.

Jenkins, Cloy. *Prologue: An Examination of Mormon Attitudes Towards Homosexuality.* Provo, UT: Prometheus Enterprises, 1978.

Johnsen, D. K. "Just One Breath" *Affinity* 13, no. 7 (1991): 3.

Jorstad, Erling. *Holding Fast; Pressing On: Religion in America in the 1980s*. New York: Praeger, 1990.

Kimball, Edward and Andrew E. Kimball. *Spencer W. Kimball*, Salt Lake City: Bookcraft, 1977.

Kimball, Spencer W. *President Kimball Speaks Out*, Salt Lake City: Deseret Book, 1981.

———. *The Miracle of Forgiveness*. Salt Lake City: Bookcraft, 1969.

Kosmin, Barry A., Egon Mayer and Ariela Keysar, *American Religious Identification Survey, 2001*. New York: The Graduate Center of the City University of New York, 2001.

Kuhn, Thomas. *The Structure of Scientific Revolutions*. Chicago: University of Chicago Press, 1962.

Lach, David Alan. *Homosexuality and Scripture*. Los Angeles: *n.p.*, 1989. A booklet published by Affirmation. A copy is in the author's files.

Le Blanc, Paul Emile. "A Question of Love," *Dialogue: A Journal of Mormon Thought* 20, no. 1 (1987): 10.

Lemert Edwin. *Social Pathology: Approach to the Theory of Sociopathic Behavior*. New York: McGraw-Hill, 1951.

Lienen, Stephen. *Gay Cops*. New Brunswick, NJ: Rutgers University Press, 1993.

Loveridge, Arnold V. "Inclining to Caring Acts" *Sunstone* 14, no. 3, (1990): 2.

Marmor, Judd. *Homosexual Behavior: A Modern Reappraisal*. New York: Basic Books, 1980.

Mauss, Armand L. *All Abraham's Children: Changing Mormon Conceptions of Race and Lineage*, Urbana, IL: University of Illinois Press, 2003.

McBride, Max Ford. *Effect of Visual Stimuli in Electric Shock Therapy*, Ph.D. Dissertation, Brigham Young University, 1976.

McGaghy, Charles H. *Deviant Behavior: Crime, Conflict, and Interest Groups*. New York: Macmillan, 1985.

McKonkie, Bruce R. *Mormon Doctrine*. Salt Lake City: Bookcraft, 1966.

Miller, Ed. *Questions that Matter*. New York: McGraw-Hill, 1984.

Miller, Gordon. "Open Letter to Members and Friends of Affirmation" in *Affirmations: A Select Anthology of Writings for Gay and Lesbian Mormons. n.p.*, 1985.

Millet, Robert L. *The Mormon Faith: A New Look at Christianity*. Salt Lake City: Shadow Mountain, 1998.

Missionary's Handbook. Salt Lake City: The Church of Jesus Christ of Latter-day Saints, 1973. A copy is in the author's files.

Mitchell, John. "Let's Communicate" *Affinity* 14 no. 11, (1992): 2.

Morris, Steve. "Growing Pains: The Familiar Path to Self-Discovery" *Affinity* 13, no. 10 (1991): 3.

Mortensen, Paul. "Revelation: A Very Personal Communication" in *Affirmations: A Select Anthology of Writings for Gay and Lesbian Mormons. n.p.*, 1985.

Myers, David G. *Social Psychology*. New York: McGraw-Hill, 1993.

Name Withheld. "Choking in the Dust," *Dialogue: A Journal of Mormon Thought* 23, no. 4 (1990): 5.

Newell, Coke. *Latter Days: A Guided Tour through Six Billion Years of Mormonism*. New York: Saint Martin's Press, 2000.

Packer, Boyd K. *Teach Ye Diligently*. Salt Lake City: Deseret Book, 1979.

Quinn, D. Michael. "Prelude to the National 'Defense of Marriage' Campaign: Civil Discrimination against Feared or Despised Minorities," *Dialogue: A Journal of Mormon Thought* 33, no. 3 (2000): 1–52.

Raynes, Marybeth and Erin Parsons. "Single Cursedness: An Overview of LDS Authorities Statements about Unmarried People," *Dialogue: A Journal of Mormon Thought* 16, no. 3 (1983): 35–45.

Rees, Robert. "Bishop Pleads Case for LDS Gays, Lesbians," *Affinity* 13, no. 10 (1991): 1.

Richard Postelwaite. "Remember Who You Are" in *Affirmations: A Select Anthology of Writings for Gay and Lesbian Mormons. n.p.*, 1985.

Roberts, Stan. "Pastoring the Farside: Making a Place for Believing Homosexuals" *Sunstone* 14, no. 1 (1990): 13.

Roof, Wade Clark and William McKinney. *American Mainline Religion: Its Changing Shape and Future*. New Brunswick, NJ: Rugters University Press, 1987.

Rosten, Leo. *Religions of America: Ferment and Faith in an Age of Crisis*. New York: Simon and Schuster, 1975.

Schow, Ron, Wayne Schow and Maybeth Raynes. *Peculiar People: Mormons and Same Sex Orientation*, Salt Lake City: Signature Books, 1991.

Shepherd, Gary and Gordon Shepherd. *Mormon Passage: A Missionary Chronicle.* Urbana, IL: University of Illinois Press, 1998.

Shepherd, Gordon and Gary Shepherd. *A Kingdom Transformed: Themes in the Development of Mormonism*. Salt Lake City: University of Utah Press.

Shipps, Jan. *Mormonism: The Story of a New Religious Tradition*, Urbana, IL: University of Illinois Press, 1985.

Scroggs, Robin. *New Testament and Homosexuality*. Minneapolis, MN: Fortress Press, 1984.

Smith, Wilford E. "Mormon Sex Standards on College Campuses, or Deal Us Out of the Sexual Revolution," *Dialogue: A Journal of Mormon Thought* 10, no. 2 (1977): 76–81.

Spong, John Shelby. *Living in Sin? A Bishop Rethinks Sexuality*. San Francisco: Harper and Row, 1988.

Stark, Rodney and Roger Finke. *Acts of Faith: Explaining the Human Side of Religion*. Berkeley, CA: University of California Press, 2000.

Stout, Jan R. "Sin and Sexuality: Psychobiology and the Development of Homosexuality." *Dialogue* 20, no. 2 (1987): 29.

Sunstone: Mormon Experience, Scholarship, Issues and Art. Salt Lake City: The Sunstone Education Foundation.

Swedin, Eric Gottfrid. *Healing Souls: Psychotherapy in the Latter-day Saint Community*. Urbana, IL: University of Illinois Press, 2003.

Tanner, Jerald and Sandra Tanner. *Mormonism: Shadow or Reality?* Salt Lake City: Modern Microfilm, 1987.

Theodorson, George A. and Achilles G. Theodorson, *A Modern Dictionary of Sociology*. New York: Barnes and Noble, 1969.

Thumma, Scott. "Negotiating a Religious Identity," *Sociological Analysis* 52, no. 4 (1991): 333–347.

Troiden, Richard R. "Homosexual Identity Development," *Journal of Adolescent Health Care* 9 (1980): 105–113.

Understanding and Helping Those Who Have Homosexual Problems. Salt Lake City: Church of Jesus Christ of Latter-day Saints, 1992. A copy is in the author's files.

Vernon, Glenn M. *Mormonism: A Sociological Perspective*. *n.p.*, 1980.

Von Wagoner, Richard S. *Mormon Polygamy: A History*, Salt Lake City: Signature Books, 1986.

Warenski, Marylin. *Patriarchs and Politics: The Plight of the Mormon Woman*. New York: McGraw-Hill, 1980.

Wells, Joel W. and William B. Kline, "Self-disclosure of Homosexual Orientation" *Journal of Social Psychology* 127 (1987): 191–197.

Woodman, Natalie Jane. "Mental Health Issues Relevant to Lesbian Women and Gay Men," *Journal of Gay and Lesbian Psychotherapy* 1, no. 1 (1989): 53–63.